Mortgage 101:
The Secret Sauce to Homebuying, Financing & Beyond

Mortgage 101:
The Secret Sauce to Homebuying, Financing & Beyond

Jacqueline Crider

Gratitude

To my girls: You are my proudest accomplishment. Never forget that you can do anything you set your mind to. When someone says you can't, do it anyway!

To my littlest one, Kat: You are truly limitless. Never let anyone step on your dreams. Dream big, go big, and always believe in yourself.

To my husband: Thank you for believing in me, even when I wasn't sure I could do it myself. Your support means everything to me.

To my Operations Manager: You are the reason everything runs smoothly. I couldn't ask for a better partner in business or a better friend. Thank you for always being there to ensure our success.

To Janelle and Winston: The Author's Voyage course was where the vision began, but your unwavering dedication turned it into reality. This book wouldn't exist without you—thank you from the bottom of my heart.

To my Beta Readers: Your time, constructive feedback, and honesty were invaluable. I'm blessed to have the best tribe of people supporting me.

To my clients, partners, tribe, and mentors: Your belief in me has shaped my success in both business and life. I'm endlessly grateful for the trust you've placed in me.

I am so blessed to help people achieve their dreams every single day. To everyone who has been part of this journey—thank you for helping me achieve mine.

Foreword

Welcome to one of the most rewarding journeys you'll ever embark on—your path to homeownership. My name is Jordan Gerard, President of My Community Mortgage, and I'm honored to serve as your guide for a moment as you prepare to dive into this incredible resource. Think of me as your usher into a stadium of knowledge, where the spotlight shines on someone extraordinary: Jacqueline Crider.

When Jacqueline asked me to write this foreword, I immediately thought of one thing—I know she will make this easy for homebuyers. Having spent over 20 years in the mortgage industry myself, I've met countless professionals, but Jacqueline stands out. Her dedication to breaking down the complexities of homeownership and empowering her clients is unmatched. As I read through this book, I was delighted to see that my belief in her was absolutely correct.

Homeownership is so much more than a financial transaction. It's a cornerstone of stability, security, and success. Yet, the journey to purchasing a home can feel overwhelming. It's often filled with unfamiliar jargon, mountains of paperwork, and decisions that can seem daunting. Fortunately, Jacqueline Crider has created *Mortgage 101: The Secret Sauce to Homebuying, Financing & Beyond* to transform that journey from intimidating to empowering.

Over her two-decade career, Jacqueline has mastered the rare ability to make even the most complicated aspects of the mortgage process accessible and actionable. This book is a step-by-step guide filled with her approachable style, deep expertise, and unwavering passion for helping others. It doesn't just teach you how to navigate the mortgage process—it gives you the "why" behind every step, empowering you to make informed and confident decisions.

Through real-life examples and insider tips, Jacqueline brings the homebuying process to life. She illuminates the challenges, mistakes, and opportunities that every prospective homeowner should understand. Her ability to seamlessly connect the technical details with personal experiences ensures that readers aren't just informed—they're inspired.

Having spent years in this industry, I've seen firsthand how overwhelming the process can be, particularly for first-time buyers. Jacqueline has a unique gift for cutting through the noise and simplifying the experience. Her journey as a young homeowner serves as a powerful reminder of the lifelong rewards that come with making informed financial decisions early.

This book isn't just for first-time buyers. Whether you're refinancing, purchasing an investment property, or simply looking to enhance your financial literacy, *Mortgage 101* has something valuable for everyone. Jacqueline blends technical expertise with relatable advice, ensuring that even the most complex topics are approachable and practical.

Reading this book feels like sitting down with a trusted mentor—someone who genuinely cares about your success. If you've ever felt intimidated by the idea of buying a home or confused by the intricacies of securing a mortgage, this book is the solution you've been waiting for. It's your invitation to take control of your homebuying journey with clarity, confidence, and excitement.

As you turn these pages, prepare to be informed, inspired, and empowered. Jacqueline Crider's *Mortgage 101* is more than a book—it's your key to unlocking one of the most rewarding investments of your life.

Welcome to the start of something extraordinary.

- *Jordan Gerard, President of My Community Mortgage*

Table of Contents:

Preface

Mortgage 101: The Secret Sauce to Home Buying, Financing & Beyond

In my 20+ years in the mortgage industry, I've seen time and again how confusing, tedious, and even intimidating mortgages can be for those setting out to buy a home. For many, a mortgage is an unseen but essential component in their journey toward homeownership, and yet, most buyers feel unprepared or overwhelmed by the details and steps involved.

This book came to life because I believe that everyone deserves access to clear, honest, and practical advice on what it takes to secure a mortgage, understand the process, and make the most informed decisions. My aim here is simple: to pull back the curtain and provide insights from within the industry that can make your experience smoother and more successful.

What makes this book unique is my commitment to providing straightforward, actionable guidance. I'm not just outlining the mortgage process – I'm sharing real stories and examples from my career, illustrating why certain steps are important and how each decision can impact your financial future. I want readers to know not just how the mortgage process works but why each part matters.

I also speak from personal experience. When I bought my first home at 22, I watched how the equity I built over the years translated into financial security and wealth, which ultimately created a sizable wealth gap between me and my brother, who waited four years longer to buy his first home. It was a lesson in the long-term benefits of homeownership, one that I hope inspires readers to make decisions that strengthen their own financial security.

If there's one thing I want you to take away from this book, it's that the mortgage process isn't an insurmountable hurdle – it's a path to one of the best investments you can make. I hope that, through this guide, you'll feel equipped with the knowledge and confidence to approach your mortgage journey with clarity, excitement, and a sense of empowerment.

So grab a coffee, settle in, and let's get started on making your homebuying journey as smooth—and enjoyable—as a PB&J.

Introduction: Why Mortgages Matter More Than You Think

Imagine this: You're sitting in your dream home, feet propped up, sipping coffee on a quiet Sunday morning. What's the secret behind this peaceful moment? It's not just the four walls around you—it's the mortgage that made it all possible. Understanding how to navigate the mortgage process can be the difference between owning that dream home and missing out. This book is your guide to mastering that journey.

I've been in the mortgage industry for over 20 years, and if there's one thing I've learned, it's that many people are overwhelmed by the process. They see it as confusing, tedious, or downright intimidating. I've sat down to write this book countless times, only to stop because I thought, "Who wants to read about mortgages?" But here's the truth: Everyone who wants to own a home should. And they should have access to clear, honest, and practical advice. That's why this book exists.

What makes this book different? I'll pull back the curtain on the industry, giving you insider knowledge, real-life examples, and actionable tips that you won't find in most other books. By the end, you'll understand what a mortgage really is, how the process works from start to finish, and why owning a home is quite possibly the greatest financial decision you'll ever make.

Why Should I Buy a Home?

Owning a home is more than just having a place to live—it's a cornerstone of financial security and personal stability. From the perspective of a mortgage expert, let me explain why buying a home is one of the best investments you can make.

Let's start with a simple question: What exactly is a mortgage? You've probably heard the term countless times, but do you really know what it means? A mortgage is a loan specifically designed for buying real estate. If you don't have the cash to buy a home outright (and let's face it, most of us don't), a mortgage helps you bridge the gap.

But why is it called a "mortgage"? The term comes from old French: "mort" meaning "dead" and "gage" meaning "pledge." In other words, it's a "dead pledge." This may sound grim, but it's actually quite logical. The deal is "dead" once the debt is paid off—a good thing. But if you can't pay, the deal dies in a bad way, and you could lose your home. That's why understanding your mortgage and managing it properly is so important.

That's why I always tell people to buy a home as soon as they can afford it. Homeownership is one of the fastest and most reliable ways to build wealth, and I'm here to help you do just that.

Chapter 1: The Mortgage Process: A Big Picture View

Navigating the mortgage process can feel like traversing a maze, but with the right roadmap, it's manageable. Your journey begins with the loan application, which you can complete in one of three ways:

- In-Person: Meet with a mortgage expert for a face-to-face interview.
- Over the Phone: Speak to a professional who will guide you through the application.
- Online: Visit a mortgage company's website and fill out the application yourself.

There's no right or wrong method—it's all about what makes you comfortable. Personally, I recommend starting with the online application. It allows you to provide as much information as you can upfront, which speeds up the process. After that, we can follow up with any questions or clarifications.

Once your application is submitted, the next step is to provide documentation that verifies your financial information. This is where many people get tripped up, and it's crucial to get it right.

The phrase "buyers are liars" may sound harsh, but it emphasizes the importance of accuracy. You might not intentionally provide incorrect information, but mistakes can happen. For example, you might state your income as $5,000 a month, but that's your take-home pay after taxes. We need to know your gross income before deductions.

Providing accurate pay stubs, tax returns, and other documents upfront will save you headaches later. Trust me—this is the time to be thorough.

Story Time: The Importance of Accurate Information

Let me tell you about Mr. Smith, a client who was eager to buy his dream home but hesitant to dive into the nitty-gritty details. Instead of completing the mortgage application upfront, he opted to give me rough estimates of his income and debts, hoping for a quick ballpark figure.

Against my better judgment, I agreed—but only on the condition that he would submit a full application by the end of the weekend.

By Monday morning, I had his completed application in hand, and when I ran the numbers through our system, the results were... surprising. The ballpark figure I'd given him based on his estimates was off—by a staggering $50,000.

I called him immediately to break the news.

"Hi, Mr. Smith," I began carefully. "We reviewed your application, and it turns out you qualify for significantly less than the original estimate."

"How much less?" he asked, his tone tinged with concern.

"Well," I said, "about $50,000 less."

The shock on his end of the line was palpable. "What?! How could it be that far off? What happened?"

"Here's the thing," I explained. "The income you originally gave me included some earnings we can't count toward your mortgage qualification, like certain bonuses. And your debt? It turned out to be higher than you remembered."

His frustration was understandable, but it was also a critical learning moment. This kind of disconnect often happens when clients rely on rough estimates. It's not about intentionally misleading information—it's just that income qualifications and debt-to-income ratios are far more nuanced than most people realize.

The Lesson

Mr. Smith's experience highlights why providing accurate information from the start is essential when applying for a mortgage. Every detail matters—down to the last cent. Overestimating your income or forgetting to include a debt can mean the difference between securing your dream home or facing an unpleasant surprise.

Here's the bottom line: trust your mortgage expert, and do the work upfront. Gather your documents, be honest about your numbers, and let the experts guide you through the process. The effort you put in early on will save you headaches later and set you up for success.

Oh, and one more thing: if your mortgage expert isn't asking for detailed information and proper documentation, that's a red flag. A good expert will always dig into the details, because your dream of homeownership depends on it.

What Happens Next?

Now that you've filled out an application and submitted your documents, what comes next? This is when we dive into the heart of the process—checking your credit, determining your qualifications, and exploring your options. Whether you're purchasing a home or refinancing an existing loan, the steps are similar. The key difference is that refinancing involves redoing the loan on a property you already own, either to secure a lower interest rate or to access cash. Some mortgage experts may pull your credit before you submit documents, while others do it afterward. Either way, these steps usually happen around the same time. (For more on refinancing, check out the "Debunking Conventional Wisdom" section at the end of the book.)

Once your mortgage expert confirms that you qualify, it's time to move forward. If you're buying a home, this means the exciting part—house hunting—begins. If you're refinancing, you'll select the best loan option and proceed from there.

Finding the Perfect Home

When purchasing a home, the next step is to find your ideal property and make an offer. If your offer is accepted, that's when the real work begins. You might wonder, "Didn't the process start when I submitted my application and documents?" Yes, but there are many steps that can only be completed once a specific property is involved. This is when we start evaluating the property to ensure it meets all necessary criteria.

Whether you're buying a new home or refinancing an existing one, there's a lot happening behind the scenes. It's like a well-orchestrated circus, with your mortgage expert acting as the ringmaster. We'll order an appraisal and title report, and your loan will head into underwriting (if it hasn't already). Don't worry if some of this mortgage jargon sounds foreign—I'll include a glossary at the back of the book to help you decipher it all.

Navigating the Details

With the property identified and everything submitted to underwriting, there are still reports to be ordered and questions that may arise. These inquiries might require you to provide additional documents or clarify specific details. If we've done our job well from the start, the extra work on your part should be minimal.

Here's a crucial piece of advice: don't try to hide anything. We will find out eventually. In today's digital age, there's a record of almost everything. With all the reports we run, any discrepancies will come to light. If you try to conceal something and we discover it, it's far worse than being upfront from the beginning. Honesty is always the best policy, and most experts can help you navigate any issues that arise.

A Cautionary Tale: The Cost of Concealing Information

Joe was thrilled to be buying his dream home—a charming property with the wraparound porch he'd always wanted. From the start, he seemed like the ideal borrower: no outstanding loans, a spotless credit report, and an unwavering confidence that everything was in order.

The process moved along smoothly, and Joe was already picturing life in his new home. All that remained was the final report—a routine but essential step. That's when everything changed.

The report revealed a significant problem: Joe was tied to an active foreclosure. Confused and concerned, we dug deeper. It turned out that years earlier, Joe had cosigned a mortgage for his father's home. His father had fallen behind on payments, and the bank was now in the process of foreclosing on the property.

When I called Joe to explain, his shock mirrored ours. "But I'm not the one living there," he protested. "That's my dad's house!"

"Yes," I explained gently, "but as a cosigner, you're equally responsible for the mortgage. The foreclosure affects you, too."

The implications were immediate and devastating. With the foreclosure on his record, Joe no longer qualified for the loan. He had to walk away from his dream home, losing not only the property but also the time, money, and emotional investment he had poured into the process.

The Lesson

Joe's heartbreaking experience serves as a powerful reminder: honesty is critical in the mortgage process. Concealing information—whether it's a cosigned loan, forgotten debt, or any

After any additional questions are answered and all necessary documents are submitted, your loan goes back into underwriting, hopefully for the last time. While it's possible for a loan to go through underwriting more than twice, a mortgage expert who knows what they're doing will typically get it done in two rounds.

Once your loan—whether for a purchase or refinance—has successfully passed all the underwriting stages, you'll receive what's known as a "clear to close" (CTC). This is a significant milestone. A CTC means that after a thorough review of all the paperwork, reports, and fact-checking, your loan is ready to close. You might notice mortgage experts or realtors celebrating on social media when they get a CTC—it's because the hard part is over. Now, all that's left is to sign the final paperwork.

Closing the Deal

The last step in this process is closing the loan. This is when you'll sign a stack of documents that might feel overwhelming—almost like you're signing away your firstborn—but in reality, it's what makes the house or loan officially yours. If you're purchasing a home, the loan typically funds on the same day you sign, meaning the money is transferred, and the deal is finalized. However, in some states, like Arizona, the loan must be recorded before it can be funded.

For those refinancing, your loan might be funded on the same day if it's for a second home or investment property. For primary residences, it generally takes about four days.

If all these terms and steps are making your head spin, don't worry—I'll break everything down in more detail soon.

Recap: The Mortgage Process in a Nutshell

To summarize:

1. You submitted an application, provided documentation, and had your credit pulled.
2. You were approved by a mortgage expert, chose your property (or already owned it), and moved into underwriting while various reports were ordered.
3. Your loan returned to underwriting as the reports came in and any additional information was provided.
4. Finally, your loan was cleared to close, you signed the paperwork, and your loan became official once it was funded.

What a whirlwind! Now, let's dive deeper into the nitty-gritty details to truly understand what each step means.

Chapter 2: The Mortgage Application: Your Financial Snapshot

Earlier, we touched on the mortgage application as part of the big picture, likening it to an interview process. Now, let's dive deeper to understand what it really is, how it works, and why it matters. The mortgage application is the cornerstone of the home-buying process. Without a solid application, the rest of the journey may hit bumps, leading to potential pitfalls. Pay close attention to the "whys" in this section—grasping them will make the rest of the process much smoother.

Why Is the Application Like an Interview?

The mortgage application—commonly referred to as the 1003 form or the Uniform Residential Loan Application—is essentially a detailed snapshot of your financial history, typically covering the last two years or more. You'll be asked questions like: Where have you lived for the past two-plus years? Where have you worked during that time? What is your income? What are your assets? But why all these questions? And why two years?

From the lender's perspective, you're asking to borrow a substantial sum of money, often three to five times your annual income. Imagine it was your money—would you lend such a large amount to someone you don't know without understanding their financial situation? You'd likely want some assurance that they could repay you, right?

That's exactly what mortgage companies are doing. They ask these questions to determine your "creditworthiness"—in simple terms, whether you appear capable, on paper, of repaying a large sum of money over time. While buying a house is deeply personal for you, it's a business transaction for the lender. They're assessing who has the best statistical likelihood of paying them back. That's why they need two years of your history and why the questions delve into so much detail—it's all about ensuring you can repay the loan. It's as straightforward as that.

The questions might seem overwhelming but don't overthink them. Be sure to include at least two years of job history. If you didn't work during that time, note "unemployed" or "in school" if applicable. And yes, a full two years is required—if you have only one year and 11 months of job history, they'll want that last month. The same goes for your residence history—provide a complete two-year record. I advise my clients to do their best to answer every question thoroughly. If you get stuck, fill out the form as best as you can and let me know where you had trouble. Hopefully, after reading this section, you'll be able to complete a mortgage application like a pro.

The Application: A Step-by-Step Guide

While different companies may organize the questions differently, I'll walk you through the questions as they typically appear on the form. If your application orders the questions differently, don't worry—it just means their process is a little different. Some companies might even ask a few extra questions they find important, so if that happens, it's just part of their process.

Individual or Joint Credit

One of the first things most applications will ask is whether you're applying individually (individual credit) or with someone else (joint credit). Technically, you can have as many people on the loan as you want, though I recommend limiting it to those who are essential. Typically, the number of applicants ranges from one to two.[1]

Story Time: How Many People Can Be on a Loan?

A while back, I worked on a particularly unique refinance. The property in question? A vacation home jointly owned by 30 people—15 couples who had pooled their resources to buy the house and split the time they could use it. Think of it as a DIY timeshare, only with the added complexity of joint ownership.

---

[1] ***Note:*** *Any words that are in* purple *are defined in the glossary in the back of the book.*

When the group decided it was time for some much-needed maintenance and upgrades, they opted for a cash-out refinance. That's when the fun began.

The plan sounded simple enough at first, but then they hit me with their request: they wanted all 15 husbands to be on the loan. Hypothetically, this was possible—there's technically no limit to the number of borrowers on a mortgage. But practically speaking? It was a recipe for chaos.

I sat down with the group to explain the challenges:

- **Debt Calculation:** Every single one of the 15 borrowers would have to disclose all their debts. This meant combing through car loans, student loans, credit cards, and any other financial obligations for all of them.
- **Document Submission:** Each borrower would need to submit a mountain of paperwork—pay stubs, tax returns, bank statements, and more. Just imagining the sheer volume of documents made my head spin.
- **Credit Score Impact:** This was the real kicker. When multiple borrowers apply for a loan, lenders use the lowest of the three middle credit scores from all applicants. All it would take was one person with a shaky credit history to drag down the entire group's qualification and possibly lead to a higher interest rate for everyone.

I pointed out that the number of loan applicants didn't determine ownership—only financing. "Instead of putting everyone on the loan," I suggested, "let's choose 2 to 4 of the strongest applicants with the best financial profiles. They can apply for the loan, and the ownership structure can remain the same."

The group agreed, and we moved forward with a much smaller, more manageable loan application team. The process went smoothly after that, and they got the cash they needed for their upgrades without unnecessary headaches.

But I can't lie—part of me still wonders what that closing would've looked like if all 30 owners had been there, pens in hand, ready to sign. It would have been a spectacle for the ages!

The Lesson

When it comes to applying for a mortgage or refinance, less is often more. The fewer applicants, the easier the process and the cleaner the final approval. Ownership doesn't depend on the loan—it's about how the title is set up. If you're in a similar situation, focus on including only the strongest financial candidates on the loan to streamline the process and improve your chances of securing favorable terms.

If you have more than one person applying for the loan, you'll repeat all steps for each applicant. If someone on the loan doesn't have a job, such as a stay-at-home spouse, that's fine—just follow the process for them too. The only time it matters who is listed first is if one of the applicants is a veteran or active-duty military member; they must go first, regardless of employment status or income. Some people ask if the highest earner should go first. The answer is no—it doesn't matter, unless military status is involved.

Your Name

When we ask for your name, we mean your legal name—not your nickname or middle name, but the name on your official documents. I often get asked whether you need to include your middle name. You don't have to, and in many cases, I recommend you don't, with a few exceptions:

- **Common Names:** If you go by your middle name or have a common name like "John Smith," including your middle initial or full middle name can help avoid confusion.
- **Name Changes:** If you're getting married and plan to change your name, use your current legal name at the time of the application. I suggest waiting to change your name until after the loan process is complete to avoid unnecessary paperwork. If you're determined to change it beforehand, talk to your mortgage expert—they'll guide you through the additional documentation needed.

Birth Date, Social Security Number, and Contact Information

Next, we'll ask for your birth date, Social Security number, phone number, and years of schooling. Your birth date is one of the simplest questions—just the month, day, and year. The Social Security number is also straightforward, but here's a tip: we verify it, so don't even think about using someone else's. We will find out.

Why do these details matter? Your birth date is a key identifier and will appear on many of the documents you submit. It also ensures we're lending to someone over the age of 18. Your Social Security number ties your credit report to your identity, ensuring that the loan application is truly yours. No one wants someone else taking out a loan in their name for hundreds of thousands of dollars, so that's why we need your Social Security number.

For those concerned about identity theft, rest assured: the mortgage industry is highly regulated. We undergo extensive background checks, fingerprinting, and licensing requirements to protect your information. For instance, I had to complete 20 hours of pre-licensing classes, pass a licensing exam, and submit my fingerprints to the federal government for background checks in multiple states. With these rigorous standards, it would be professional suicide for any of us to consider stealing your identity.

Marital Status

The next question is about your marital status. You'll have three options: married, separated, or unmarried. If you're divorced, you're unmarried. If you're single, you're unmarried. "Separated" refers to a legal separation, and it's important to note that not all states recognize legal separation. If you're not legally separated but still married, mark "married." Just make sure to inform your mortgage expert if you're getting divorced or are in the process of a divorce.

Why does marital status matter? In some states, like Texas, community property laws apply. If you're married and buying a house without including your spouse on the loan, that's fine—but there may be paperwork your spouse will need to sign due to these laws. We'll cover community property laws in more detail later.

Dependents

You'll also be asked about the number of dependents you have and their ages. This includes only those not listed under another applicant on the application. A dependent is anyone you claim on your tax return, which could include children, parents, siblings, etc.

Why do we care about dependents? While it might not affect every loan product, some products consider this information relevant, so we ask upfront.

Dependent Story: The Importance of Accuracy

One loan product that cares about dependents is the VA loan. Early in my career, I was working on a VA loan for a really sweet family with a bunch of kids. The applicant marked on his application that he had four dependents, which made sense since we had talked at length about his four children. However, when underwriting requested a copy of his tax return to verify, it turned out he also claimed his father, who lived with them, as a dependent.

Because of how the VA underwrites loans, this almost derailed the entire process. Fortunately, as a seasoned expert, I was able to navigate through some hoops and still make the loan work. That experience taught me the critical importance of answering the dependents question accurately.

Address Information

- **Present Address:** This is your current living address, where you regularly stay. It helps verify your stability and residency history, both of which are crucial in assessing your financial stability.
- **Mailing Address:** Where you receive mail. This could be a P.O. Box, a family member's address, or another location where you get correspondence. Ensuring we have the

correct mailing address is important for sending you vital documents and verifying any discrepancies that might arise.

- **Rent or Own:** This question determines whether you rent or own your current residence. If you live rent-free, you should still select "rent." Owning a home previously often positively influences your application.
- **Length of Time at Present Address:** How long you've lived at your current address in years and months. This helps us understand your stability over time. We need a full two years of history, but exact months aren't required if the duration is extensive.

Employment Information

- **Employer Name and Address:** The company name that appears on your paycheck or tax documents. If you're unsure, ask your boss. This information is crucial for verifying your employment status.
- **Self-Employed:** Check this if you own your business or receive a 1099 form. If you're not sure, generally, if no federal taxes are withheld from your pay, you're considered self-employed. This helps classify your employment correctly for an accurate financial assessment.
- **Years at Job:** How long you've been at your current job? This provides a measure of employment stability. Be precise with the number of years and months.

- **Years in Line of Work/Profession:** Total time you've worked in your profession, regardless of the employer. This indicates your overall experience in your field, even if you've changed jobs.
- **Position/Title/Type of Business:** Your specific job title and the type of business you work in. If self-employed, include your position and business type. This information aids in evaluating your income and stability.
- **Business Phone Number:** A number where we can verify your employment. This could be the company's main line or the HR department. It's essential for confirming your employment details.

Understanding the Importance of Your Financial Picture

- **Risk and Reward**

  Mortgage lenders need to ensure they can recover their investment, plus interest, when they lend money. If your income or job stability is questionable, it poses a risk. Just like you wouldn't lend money to someone without knowing they can repay you, lenders need to assess your financial reliability.

- **Painting a Financial Picture**

  Think of the application process as painting a picture of your financial situation. This includes showing your income stability, job history, and any reasons for gaps or changes. The goal is to help the lender understand your overall financial health.

- ○ **Addressing Imperfections**

  If there are any gaps or inconsistencies in your employment or income, it's important to explain them. For example, if you're returning to work after a break or have recently changed jobs, provide a clear explanation.

Common Concerns and Solutions

- **Job Stability:** If you haven't been in your job for long, explain why. For instance, if you recently completed your education or returned to work after a break, this is relevant information. If you've changed jobs within the same profession, highlight your career progression and stability in the field.
- **Income Variability:** If you've recently started a new job with a higher salary, lenders may still use your new income to qualify you, though they might exclude bonuses or commissions initially. Clearly state whether you're salaried or hourly, and calculate your income accurately based on your pay structure.

Practical Examples

- **Veterinarian Case:** A veterinarian was able to buy a house before starting a new job by using a job offer letter and meeting employment conditions. Job start dates aren't always a barrier if other conditions are met.
- **Physician's Assistant Case:** A physician's assistant with unconventional income documentation was able to get a loan by providing a written verification of employment from her employer. Therefore, alternative documentation can be a solution to income challenges.

Income Calculation Tips

- **Salaried Employees:** Enter your annual salary or divide it by 12 to get your monthly income. Do not deduct taxes or other withholdings.
- **Hourly Employees:**
    - **Simple Calculation:** Multiply your hourly rate by the number of hours you work per week, then by 4.33 (weeks per month).
    - **Detailed Calculation:** Multiply your hourly rate by 40 hours per week, then by 52 weeks per year, and divide by 12.

By providing a clear and accurate picture of your financial situation and explaining any potential issues, you'll help the lender understand your ability to repay the loan. Remember, each financial situation is unique, and persistence often leads to finding a solution that works for you.

Part-Time Income: What You Need to Know

One of the critical things to keep in mind is that part-time income is rarely usable unless you've held the part-time job for at least two years. This applies to any part-time position or seasonal job you might have. If you're working part-time or in a seasonal role, your income from these jobs will likely only count if you've been employed in that capacity for a minimum of two years. There are exceptions to this rule, so it's crucial to discuss your specific situation with your mortgage expert.

Bonuses, Commissions, and Overtime: How They Affect Your Application

You might be wondering, "What if I get bonuses, commissions, or overtime?" The answer isn't straightforward—it depends heavily on how consistently you receive these payments. It's not necessary to get a bonus every month or receive the same exact commission or overtime each time, but there must be some stability in this income.

Here's what that means: If you've been receiving bonuses, commissions, or overtime for the last two years or more, and the amounts are either consistent or increasing, we should be able to use this income, provided you're still with the same employer. However, if these numbers have been decreasing, we may only be able to use part of this income—or possibly none at all. This is where an experienced mortgage expert comes in; they will review your documents and help you understand how much of this income can be used.

If you're trying to calculate your income for the application, the easiest method is to estimate how much bonus, commission, or overtime you've received over the last two years and divide that by 24 months. This will give you a rough monthly amount. While it might not be exact, your mortgage expert will help fine-tune these numbers.

Story Time: The Importance of Stability with Overtime Income

When it comes to securing a mortgage, stability is everything. Let me tell you about a client, James, who learned this lesson the hard way.

James was a hard-working guy who regularly clocked 20 hours of overtime each week. His dedication paid off—not only with a bigger paycheck but also by strengthening his mortgage application. Because his overtime was consistent, we could confidently include it as part of his income, significantly boosting the amount he qualified for. Things were looking great, and he was thrilled to be under contract for his dream home.

During one of our check-ins, James casually mentioned that he was considering changing jobs. It was a better position, with a higher base salary but less predictable over time. Alarm bells went off immediately.

"James," I cautioned, "please wait until after closing to make any changes. Your current overtime income is key to your qualification. If you switch jobs now, we might not be able to use it—and that could jeopardize everything."

He nodded and assured me he'd think it over. But just a few weeks later, I got the news: James had taken the new job. He assumed we wouldn't find out, thinking his higher salary would make up for the loss of overtime. Unfortunately, that's not how mortgages work.

When we reevaluated his application, we had to remove the overtime income entirely. Without it, James no longer qualified for the loan. It was devastating—for him and for us. He lost the $20,000 he'd put down as earnest money and, worst of all, his dream home slipped through his fingers.

It was a heartbreaking outcome, made even more frustrating because it was 100% avoidable. If James had waited just a few more weeks to change jobs, everything would have been fine. The deal would have closed, and he could have made the career move without risking his home purchase.

The Lesson

When you're in the middle of the mortgage process, any changes to your job or income can have serious consequences. Even if the change seems like an improvement, lenders need to see stability and predictability. That means keeping things steady until after closing day.

If you're thinking about making a big move—whether it's a new job, changing your income structure, or taking on new debt—talk to your mortgage expert first. A few weeks of patience could save you from losing your home and your hard-earned money.

"Other" Income: What It Includes and How to Report It

Next up on the application is a section labeled "Other Income." This can include retirement, Social Security, disability, alimony, child support, separate maintenance, etc. Though it may seem odd to lump all of these income types together, that's how they're often categorized.

When entering these amounts, be sure to report the income before any deductions—before federal or state taxes, insurance (including Medicaid), or anything else is taken out. You are not required to disclose alimony, child support, or separate maintenance unless you want it considered for loan qualification. However, if you do include it, you must be receiving these payments for at least three more years for them to be counted as income.

Since most of these types of income are received monthly, just enter the monthly amount. Don't shortchange yourself by entering the amount after deductions—if you're unsure, you can refer to your annual award letter (which we'll need later for documentation anyway).

Self-Employment Income:

If you're self-employed, things get a bit more complicated. The best approach is to submit two full years of personal and business tax returns and let your mortgage team analyze them. Why? Because calculating self-employment income involves intricate details, much of which depends on how your tax preparer structured your taxes. If you're into math or just curious, I'll provide a link later in the book where you can plug in your tax return numbers to get an estimate of the income we can use.

If your income isn't easily provable through pay stubs, W-2s/1099s, or tax returns, don't worry—there are options, like non-QM loans or bank statement loan products, which I'll discuss later. These out-of-the-box solutions can help you qualify for a mortgage even if you don't fit the traditional mold.

Story Time: Non-Traditional Income and Bank Statement Loans

Sometimes, clients don't fit neatly into the standard mortgage process—but that doesn't mean their dreams are out of reach. One such client, Lisa, ran a successful event planning business. Her income was substantial, but her tax returns told a different story. Like many self-employed individuals, Lisa used legal deductions to minimize her taxable income, which unfortunately made it difficult to qualify for a traditional mortgage.

Lisa was frustrated. "I make great money," she said during our consultation. "But my tax returns make it look like I'm barely scraping by. What can I do?"

Fortunately, there was a solution: a bank statement loan. Instead of relying on her tax returns, this loan product allowed us to use the income reflected in her business bank accounts to determine her eligibility. It was the perfect fit for Lisa's situation, but the process came with its own hurdles.

As we reviewed Lisa's bank statements, we discovered a challenge: multiple non-sufficient funds (NSF) fees. These occur when there isn't enough money in the account to cover a transaction, and they're a red flag for lenders. While the occasional NSF might be overlooked, Lisa's statements showed a pattern that could make her application problematic.

When I explained this to her, she was initially deflated. "Does this mean I can't qualify?" she asked.

"Not necessarily," I reassured her. "We'll need to get creative, but I've seen situations like this work out before. It just takes some extra effort—and honesty."

Together, we tackled the issue head-on. Lisa provided detailed explanations for the NSFs, showing they were tied to large, one-time expenses for her business. Additionally, we worked to highlight her consistent deposits, which clearly demonstrated her earning power. By focusing on the overall strength of her financial profile, we were able to present a compelling case to the lender.

In the end, Lisa's persistence—and willingness to work through the obstacles—paid off. She secured the loan, closed on her dream home, and gained valuable insights into managing her finances along the way.

The Lesson

If you don't qualify for a traditional loan, don't lose hope. Non-traditional solutions, like bank statement loans, are designed for people whose financial situations don't align with conventional guidelines. But be prepared to show the full picture of your finances and work with an expert who understands the nuances of these loan products.

Challenges like NSFs can be navigated, but only if you're upfront and willing to address them. With the right guidance, even unconventional paths can lead you to your dream home.

Why Income Stability Matters

The key takeaway here is that lenders need to see stable income to ensure you can repay the loan. They don't have a crystal ball to predict your financial future, so they rely on your past two years of income history to gauge stability. This is why bonuses, commissions, and overtime are scrutinized—if these income sources are likely to stop soon, including them in your overall income could jeopardize your ability to repay the loan.

Remember, lenders only make money if you make your monthly payments. They, like you, have a vested interest in your financial stability. While some of the rules might seem strict or even unfair, they're in place to protect both you and the lender from financial hardship.

Assets: What They Are and How to Report Them

Now let's talk about assets, often referred to as "money honey." Assets include anything you can quickly convert into cash, such as checking and savings accounts, stocks, bonds, 401(k)s, IRAs, and life insurance with significant cash values.

A Word to the Wise: You'll need to provide documentation for each asset, so it's often best not to list every account if they contain minimal amounts. Focus on your biggest, most significant assets—those that will play a key role in your down payment or refinancing plans.

Story Time: The Perils of Overcomplicating Assets

Let me introduce you to Sarah, a client who was excited to secure a mortgage for her dream home. On paper, Sarah's financial profile was solid—she had more than enough money to cover her down payment, closing costs, and even a comfortable cushion for future expenses. The issue? Her assets were spread across 15 different accounts.

Sarah had checking accounts, savings accounts, investment accounts, and even a few accounts she'd forgotten about until we asked her for statements. To make things more complicated, she frequently moved money between these accounts—sometimes to cover bills, other times to take advantage of small interest rate differences. While this might have worked fine for her personal financial strategy, it created a logistical nightmare for her mortgage application.

Every single transaction needed to be documented. Was the money a gift? A loan? A reimbursement? And because many of the transactions weren't direct deposits, we had to dig deeper into their origins. Each transfer required additional paperwork—statements from both the sending and receiving accounts. What could have been a straightforward process turned into a marathon of sourcing funds.

"Why does this matter so much?" Sarah asked one afternoon, clearly exasperated by the back-and-forth.

I explained, "Lenders are required to trace all the funds you're using for your mortgage to ensure they're legitimate. If the money moves too much or comes from an unknown source, it raises questions and can delay your approval—or worse, derail it entirely."

She paused and sighed. "So, what could I have done differently?"

I smiled. "Honestly? Consolidating your funds into one or two main accounts at least 60 days before applying would have saved us all a lot of time and stress."

This wasn't an option for Sarah at this stage, so we powered through, documenting every deposit and transfer until her file was finally complete. After what felt like an endless paper trail, her loan was approved, and she closed on her home.

The Lesson

When it comes to applying for a mortgage, simplicity is your best friend. Consolidate your assets into one or two accounts well before you apply—ideally 60 to 90 days in advance. This will minimize the need for extensive documentation and make the process smoother for both you and your lender.

While Sarah's story had a happy ending, the stress and extra work could have been avoided with a little preparation. So, if you're planning to buy a home, take a good look at your accounts and ask yourself: could simplifying them save me—and my mortgage expert—a major headache?

Disclosure of Property and Asset Information

When completing this section, it's essential to disclose any properties you own. It's important to be transparent—if you own a property, tell us upfront. We run comprehensive reports, so any undisclosed assets will eventually come to light. Avoid unnecessary complications by being honest from the start.

Regarding vehicles, although they were once commonly listed as assets, it's generally not recommended today due to the complexities involved. Most online applications no longer require this, but if one does, consider whether it's worth the effort of proving its value and associated loans.

For your assets, accuracy is key. Include the bank or financial institution's name and an approximate figure for each account. It doesn't need to be exact but try to be reasonably close. You'll eventually need to provide proof, so accurate ballpark figures are ideal. Avoid moving your money around during this time—it complicates the process and can create unnecessary headaches.

Here's a real-world example: A client decided to move money between accounts just before applying for a mortgage. Although she had valid reasons, we had to track each transfer and provide detailed documentation, all because of stringent anti-money laundering regulations. Every account involved needed two months of statements, and we had to source every deposit. Pro tip: If the transaction occurred more than 60 days ago and you're not using a bank statement loan, it won't be scrutinized.

The best strategy is to keep your main assets in an account with minimal activity, especially if you're planning to buy a home soon. Parking the funds in one account for 60-90 days with little movement will minimize paperwork and streamline the process.

Why Assets Matter

For a home purchase, assets are straightforward—we need to verify that you have enough for the down payment and closing costs. For a refinance, it's about stability—do you have a financial cushion? While there isn't a strict asset requirement, having them helps us understand your financial situation and explore various qualification options.

When listing assets, focus on the major ones—retirement accounts, significant stock holdings, and your primary savings account. You don't need to list every account, just the ones with substantial value.

The Importance of the Loan Application

Your loan application is the foundation of our decision-making process. A great mortgage expert will ensure it's accurate, but understanding why these sections matter helps you avoid unnecessary stress and delays. This is a significant purchase, and getting it right the first time is crucial to minimize frustration.

Two Stories: A Lesson in Planning

Story One: The Cost of Last-Minute Decisions

On a Saturday morning, I got a panicked call from a client, Alex. He had just toured what he described as his "absolute dream home"—the kind of place he'd been imagining for years. There was just one problem: Alex hadn't checked if he could afford it.

He needed a pre-approval letter *immediately* to make an offer before someone else scooped up the property. Normally, we aim to turn around pre-approvals within 24-48 hours, but Alex didn't have that kind of time. We scrambled to review his application and documents, rushing through what would normally be a careful and thorough process.

As we dug into his financials, the cracks started to show. There were negative items on his credit report—things he hadn't mentioned and likely didn't even realize were there. These items disqualified him from securing the pre-approval he needed. The disappointment in his voice was palpable when I delivered the news.

"If only I'd known earlier," he muttered.

Had Alex consulted us weeks earlier, we could have helped him address the credit issues and put together a solid plan. Instead, his dream home slipped through his fingers, all because of a lack of preparation.

Story Two: The Power of Early Preparation

Contrast Alex's experience with another couple, Emily and Mark. When they decided they were ready to buy a home, their first call wasn't to a realtor—it was to us.

"We're thinking of buying in a few months," Emily said. "What do we need to do to get ready?"

This proactive approach made all the difference. Over the next few weeks, Emily and Mark carefully filled out their application, gathered the necessary documents, and gave us plenty of time to review everything. In the process, we identified a couple of minor issues—nothing disqualifying, but things that could be improved to strengthen their application.

Because they started early, we had time to address those issues, ensuring their financial profile was rock solid by the time they began house hunting. When they finally found their dream home, their offer was backed by a pre-approval letter that gave the seller confidence. Emily and Mark closed on their home without a single hitch—and with far less stress than Alex experienced.

The Difference? Planning.

These two stories show just how critical planning is in the home-buying process. Giving your mortgage expert the time to do their job thoroughly ensures a smoother experience and better results.

If you're thinking about buying a home, don't wait until the last minute to get pre-approved. Start early, be proactive, and let your mortgage expert guide you. Your future self—and your dream home—will thank you.

Final Thoughts

As you wrap up the application, most of the remaining sections should be straightforward. For the liabilities section, there's no need to list every debt manually—we'll pull your credit report to verify your debts. However, if you have significant obligations not listed on your report, such as alimony or child support, be sure to disclose them. Being thorough from the start helps prevent surprises later on.

In the real estate section, if you don't own any property, this will be a quick step. Remember that "property" includes land, not just homes. For example, a client once forgot to mention a piece of land gifted by his father, which caused unnecessary stress when it showed up later. Transparency here is key to avoiding similar issues.

Next, you'll encounter a series of disclosure questions. The first batch covers things like whether you're a co-signer on any loans that might not appear on your credit report or if you've had a bankruptcy in the past seven years. Answer these to the best of your ability. If you're uncertain about anything, just let your mortgage expert know—they're there to help you correct any inaccuracies.

The second batch of questions relates to military service. We ask these to determine if you might qualify for special military financing options. Finally, you'll reach the demographic questions. These questions are required because the mortgage industry is federally monitored to ensure fair lending practices. The information is collected to make sure loan companies aren't denying credit based on race, gender, or other protected characteristics.

To put it simply, as long as your financials are in order, nothing else matters to us. All mortgage experts worth their salt focus on helping you secure the loan, regardless of your background. You can choose whether or not to answer the demographic questions, as they're entirely optional. Their purpose is to ensure fairness in the lending process.

If at any point you feel you're being treated unfairly, please don't hesitate to reach out to me or my team. Our goal is to make homeownership accessible to everyone. It's frustrating that discrimination still exists, but I assure you that we are committed to providing the highest level of service to all clients.

So, there you have it. Filling out the application isn't difficult—it's just about following instructions and being honest. If you're prone to overthinking, try not to stress. Fill out the form, use my tips, and move on. If you've chosen a great expert, you're in good hands.

Now that you've filled out the application and hit submit, what happens next? Here's what to expect...

Chapter 3: Submit Documents

Remember how I mentioned that you'd need to provide documentation? Let's dive into what you'll need to submit, why it's important, and why it matters so much. By now, you probably have an idea of the types of documents we'll ask for based on the earlier parts of the application. But let's walk through it together to make sure everything is clear. The hardest part of the mortgage process is often the upfront work of gathering these documents. While it may not be fun, the good news is that once this is done, most of the heavy lifting falls on your mortgage expert.

Why Documents Matter

You're not asking to borrow a small sum of money—this is a significant amount, and the company lending it to you wants to ensure they're making a sound investment. They're asking for documents to verify everything you've put down on the almighty application. It's a reasonable request, right? I mean, would you lend someone half a million dollars without checking their financials? I know I wouldn't.

Some people mistakenly believe that the mortgage process is like buying a car: you walk in, share a few details, they check your credit, and you're good to go. Mortgage lending is much more thorough. A good mortgage expert will try to simplify the process as much as possible—after all, that's what my company, PBJ Mortgage, stands for: "making mortgage simple, as simple as making a peanut butter and jelly sandwich." But even though we aim to make it simple, we still have to follow the rules, guidelines, and laws that govern the mortgage industry.

If you're wondering why there's so much paperwork and red tape in mortgage lending, you can thank the fraudsters and shady dealings that occurred before 2008. A mountain of regulations came into place to tighten things up after that. So, that's why these documents matter so much. I'm going to walk you through the most commonly requested documents, the less common ones, and some of the most frequent mistakes we see—along with a few stories to illustrate my points.

Commonly Requested Documents

First, let's talk about the information you gave us about your job and income. We have to document that. Thankfully, most of this information is available electronically, which should make the process easier.

Pay Stubs: Most people are familiar with pay stubs—they detail how much you're paid and when. If you work a regular, non-self-employed job, you likely get paid in one of three ways: bi-weekly (every other week), semi-monthly (typically on the 15th and

30th/1st), or monthly. Some people are paid weekly, but that's less common. You'll need to provide 30 days' worth of pay stubs. Here's what that looks like:

- **Weekly Pay:** 5 pay stubs
- **Bi-weekly Pay:** 3 pay stubs
- **Semi-monthly Pay:** 2 pay stubs
- **Monthly Pay:** 1 pay stub

If you're unsure, check the dates on your pay stubs—they'll tell you how often you're paid.

Bank Statements: We need these to prove how much money you actually have in your bank accounts. It's crucial to only provide statements for the accounts you listed on your application. This is why I advised earlier that you might want to limit the number of accounts you include. Providing statements for multiple accounts can turn into a paperwork nightmare. We require two full months of statements, and most banks issue statements monthly. If your bank operates on a different schedule, just ensure you provide two full months' worth.

Story Time: When Too Much is Too Much

Let me tell you about Claire, a client who was determined to be as thorough as possible during her mortgage application process. Claire had a habit of keeping her finances meticulously organized, and as part of her application, she wanted to include every single bank account she owned.

When we reviewed her application, we noticed she had listed a total of 15 accounts. Naturally, we asked for two months of statements for each one. Claire was shocked—she hadn't realized that providing paperwork for all 15 accounts would be such a monumental task.

After some discussion, we assured her that it wasn't necessary to include every single account. A few hundred dollars here and there in smaller accounts usually won't make or break an application. Instead, we narrowed it down to 2-3 major accounts that showcased her financial strength and met the underwriting requirements.

With this streamlined approach, Claire's application became far more manageable, and the process moved forward smoothly.

The Lesson

When it comes to your mortgage application, you don't need to include every single detail about your finances unless specifically requested. Focusing on your main accounts is often enough to meet the requirements and keep the process efficient.

If something critical is missing, your mortgage expert will let you know. Trust their guidance to save yourself time and unnecessary

Why These Documents Are Important

Documents like pay stubs and bank statements aren't just formalities—they're crucial for verifying your financial stability. When you apply for a mortgage, you're essentially asking the lender to make a significant investment in you. They need to ensure you can handle the responsibility. Gathering these documents might seem tedious, but it's a necessary part of the process.

Driver's License or Government-Issued ID

Next up is your driver's license or a valid government-issued ID. This one is simple: we need a copy of your ID to verify your identity. It must be unexpired, and we require either a scanned copy or a very clear picture. A tip: keep a clear image of your ID saved on your phone in case you ever lose it. This document is required for everyone listed on the loan, so make sure it's easily accessible.

W-2s: Two Years of Income Verification

Now we're getting into documents that may take a bit more effort to find. You'll need two years' worth of W-2s. The W-2 is the form you receive in January or early February each year, detailing the money you made at your job the previous year. It's also the form you use to prepare your taxes. If you receive your paystubs electronically, you can usually access your W-2s the same way.

It's important to note that this includes W-2s from any job you've worked in the last two years, even if you didn't list the job on your application. For example, if you had a small part-time job that issued a W-2, you still need to include it.

Retirement and Stock Account Statements

You'll also need to provide statements for any retirement or stock accounts you listed on your application. If you didn't include them because they have minimal funds, you won't need to provide statements. Most retirement accounts issue quarterly statements, so you'll only need one statement. If the account issues monthly statements, you'll need two full months' worth. These can usually be accessed through your online portal.

Tax Returns: The Full Picture

The last commonly requested document is two years of personal federal tax returns. Here are a few things to remember:

- **All Pages and Schedules:** We need the complete federal return—no state returns necessary.
- **Timing:** If you're applying early in the year and haven't yet filed your taxes for the previous year, that's okay. Prior to April 15th, you don't need to provide the previous year's return. If you've already filed, go ahead and include it.
- **Extensions:** If you've filed for an extension, provide the two years before and the extension letter.

These returns are vital for painting a complete picture of your financial situation. If you can't find them, your tax preparer likely has copies, or you can access them online if you used tax software. If all else fails, you can request tax transcripts—just reach out to your mortgage expert for guidance.

Special Cases: Self-Employed, Military, Retired, and More

Now that we've covered the documents most customers need, let's talk about additional paperwork required for those who are self-employed, retired, in the military, or own other properties. If you don't think this applies to you, feel free to skip ahead. But if you're unsure, contact your mortgage expert—they'll help you determine what's needed. Most systems will prompt you for the necessary documents, but it's always good to have a clear understanding yourself.

Business Tax Returns: If you own a business, you'll need to provide two years of business tax returns, including all schedules. It's crucial to submit the entire return, as missing forms can cause delays. For example, one client forgot to include the K-1 form, which indicates how much of the business he owned. This form was essential because it determined how much of the business income he could use. Without it, we couldn't proceed. So, be sure to provide the full set of documents.

1099 Forms: If you receive 1099 forms, you're considered self-employed, even if you don't think of yourself that way. These forms indicate that you're contract labor, meaning your employer doesn't withhold federal taxes, Social Security, or FICA from your pay. Just like with W-2s, you'll need to provide the two most recent years of 1099s from all employers.

Story Time: The Mountain of 1099s

Meet Jess, a dynamic public speaker whose career took her across the U.S., delivering workshops, keynotes, and seminars for a variety of organizations. Her passion for her work was evident, but when it came time to apply for a mortgage, her income documentation presented a unique challenge.

Jess was self-employed, which meant she didn't receive regular pay stubs like a traditional employee. Instead, she was issued a 1099 from every organization she worked with—dozens of them over the years. As part of the loan process, she needed to provide two years' worth of 1099s to document her income.

When Jess handed us her paperwork, it wasn't just a few forms—it was a mountain of 1099s. Some were from major corporations, others from small nonprofits, and a handful from one-off speaking engagements. The sheer volume was daunting, but Jess' meticulous organization turned what could have been a logistical nightmare into a manageable task.

She had sorted her 1099s by year, clearly labeled each one, and included a summary sheet with the totals. This made it easy for us to cross-reference the forms with her tax returns and bank statements.

"Wow," I said, impressed by her preparation. "This is a textbook example of how to do it right."

Despite the complexity of her financial profile, we successfully processed Jess' loan because she had taken the time to organize her documents. She closed on her dream home without a hitch— and with a sense of accomplishment for tackling what many find to be an overwhelming process.

The Lesson

If you're self-employed or work in a gig economy, documentation is key. Lenders need to see a clear picture of your income, which often means gathering and organizing multiple years of 1099s, tax returns, and bank statements.

Take a page from Jess' book: stay organized, label everything, and consider creating a summary of your documents. The effort you put in upfront will make the process smoother for you and your mortgage expert—and it could mean the difference between delays and an on-time closing.

Military Service: Active Duty and Veterans

If you're on active duty or a veteran, you'll need your Certificate of Eligibility (COE) and your DD214. The DD214 is a document that almost all military personnel are familiar with. If you're on active duty and don't know where yours is, ask your command—they can help you locate it. The COE is something you can request, and it tells us if you're eligible for a VA loan. Not everyone who has served is eligible, which is why this form is so important. If you have any issues obtaining these forms, get with your mortgage expert. Those who do a lot of VA loans, like myself and my team, have resources to help you.

Story Time: The Importance of Getting Your COE Early

Let me tell you about Mike, a proud veteran who had served in the Army Reserves. When Mike decided it was time to buy a home, he was excited to use his VA loan benefits—one of the key rewards for his service. But as we started the process, we hit an unexpected snag: Mike's Certificate of Eligibility (COE), the document verifying his VA loan eligibility, wasn't available in the electronic system.

"Not a problem," I reassured him. "We'll request it by mail. It might take a little longer, but we'll keep things moving in the meantime."

Mike got under contract for a house, and we reminded him repeatedly that the COE was critical for moving forward. He brushed it off, confident that his service record would qualify him. Based on everything Mike had shared about his time in the Reserves, we believed him, so we continued processing the loan, trusting the COE would confirm his eligibility.

Weeks later, the COE finally arrived—and it wasn't the news anyone expected. Mike wasn't eligible for a VA loan. Why? Years earlier, he had missed attending the last two days of a drill. Those two days left him just shy of the required service time to qualify for VA benefits.

The realization hit Mike like a ton of bricks. "I had no idea those two days would matter," he said, clearly upset.

The timing couldn't have been worse. With the closing date fast approaching, we had to scramble to find a different loan option that didn't rely on his veteran status. Thankfully, we were able to pivot, and Mike qualified for a conventional loan. While he was relieved to close on his home, the stress of last-minute changes—and the additional costs that came with them—could have been entirely avoided.

The Lesson

If you're planning to use a VA loan, make your Certificate of Eligibility (COE) a top priority. Don't assume your service record automatically qualifies you—confirm it early to avoid surprises.

Your mortgage expert can help you request the COE and navigate any issues that arise, but the sooner you start this process, the smoother your journey will be. As Mike's experience shows, even small details from years ago can make a big difference. By getting your COE upfront, you'll save yourself time, stress, and potential setbacks on your path to homeownership.

Additional Documents for Property Owners

If you own other properties, you'll need to provide the following:

- **Mortgage Statements:** For any property you own with a mortgage, provide statements for each mortgage. If you own a property outright, you'll need to prove it has no mortgage.

- **Homeowners Insurance (HOI) Documents:** Provide the statement showing how much you pay. If you're refinancing, also provide the insurance declaration page. If you don't have insurance, you may need to sign a waiver.

- **Homeowners Association (HOA) Documents:** If your property is part of an HOA, provide the statement showing the amount owed, the property address, and how often payments are made.

- **Property Tax Documents:** Provide tax statements for every property you own. These are often overlooked, especially with land, but they're essential.

Story Time: The Hidden Land

Let me introduce you to David, a young professional excited to pre-qualify for his very first home. Like many first-time buyers, David was eager to make the process as smooth as possible. He provided all the necessary documents, answered every question, and seemed well on his way to pre-approval.

However, during the final review of his application, something unexpected appeared in the property report: David owned land.

When I called him to discuss it, he sounded genuinely confused. "Wait, what land?" But after a moment exclaimed, "Oh! You mean the land my dad gave me last year? I didn't think that counted."

It turned out that David's father had gifted him a small parcel of land in a rural area—a thoughtful gesture, but one David had forgotten to mention. Thankfully, in this case, the land didn't cause any significant issues. However, it easily could have. Ownership of additional property can affect a mortgage application in several ways, including tax liabilities, maintenance obligations, or even outstanding debts tied to the property.

In David's case, the land was free and clear, so it didn't impact his ability to pre-qualify. After some consideration, he decided to sell the land to simplify his financial picture. The proceeds from the sale actually helped him increase his down payment, strengthening his overall loan application.

While David's story had a happy ending, not everyone is so lucky. Failing to disclose property ownership upfront can delay the process or even disqualify you from a loan if the financial implications aren't addressed early.

The Lesson

Transparency is key when applying for a mortgage. Even if you think a property isn't relevant—like gifted land or an inherited parcel—disclose it to your mortgage expert. We're here to help, not to judge, and having all the information upfront ensures there are no surprises during the application process.

Whether the property is an asset or a liability, knowing about it early allows us to strategize effectively and set you up for success. So, take a moment to reflect: is there any property you might have forgotten about? If so, let us know—it could save you time, stress, and potential complications down the line.

Documents for Retirees

For those who are retired, you'll need to provide award letters, pension statements, Social Security statements, and possibly 1098 forms.

- **Award Letters:** These are issued annually, typically by the Social Security Administration, showing how much you'll receive in the following year. If you don't have one, you can request a copy or provide a 1098 form, which shows what was paid to you the previous year.
- **Pension Statements:** These indicate your pension amount for the current year. Some pensions send these monthly, but any recent statement will do.
- **Annuity Statements:** If you receive an annuity, provide a statement showing it will continue for at least three more years.

End-of-Year Paystubs

If you have heavy commission income, large bonuses, or significant overtime, you may need to provide end-of-year pay stubs for the prior two years. This helps us determine how much of your income is stable and consistent. While W-2s don't break out different types of income, these paystubs do, which is why they're essential for accurately calculating your qualifying income.

The Lighter Side: Common Document Mistakes (and the Stories Behind Them) or The Fun Part: Common Mistakes and Lessons Learned

I know we've been deep in the weeds with these document details, but trust me, it's all necessary. After all, these documents are proof that what you've told us is accurate, and they help us understand exactly what kind of income and assets we can use. Now, let's dive into something a bit more entertaining—common mistakes people make. Why is this fun? Because I've got stories that will not only make you chuckle but also help you avoid these pitfalls.

Mistake #1: Missing Bank Statement Pages

This is so common that you've probably seen loan officers venting about it on social media. You might have wondered why they're so worked up—well, here's why…

Story Time: Missing Pages

We once worked with Jennifer, a busy professional who preferred to complete her mortgage application over the phone. She was efficient and quick, providing all the information we needed during the call. When it came to submitting her bank statements, I explained, "Jennifer, we'll need every single page, even the blank ones. Lenders require this for compliance, so it's really important."

"No problem," she replied confidently. "I'll send them over tonight."

True to her word, the documents arrived promptly. But as I started reviewing them, I noticed something was missing—several pages were absent. I gave Jennifer a quick call to follow up.

"Hi, Jennifer," I said. "Thanks for sending over your bank statements, but I noticed a few pages are missing."

"Really?" she asked, surprised. "But those were blank pages. I didn't think you needed them."

This is a common misunderstanding, so I explained: "It might seem silly, but we need every page, even the blank ones. Otherwise, it can look like there's something missing—or worse, something being hidden. It's just part of the compliance process to ensure everything is accounted for."

Jennifer chuckled, half-amused and half-bewildered. "Blank pages? Really?"

"Yes, really!" I laughed. "It's not about what's on the page—it's about showing that nothing is missing."

She quickly sent over the remaining pages, and we were able to move forward without any issues. But the situation highlighted a common problem: clients often think they're helping by excluding seemingly unnecessary pages, when in reality, it creates more work and delays the process.

The Lesson

When it comes to mortgage documentation, more is better. Always include every page of your bank statements, even the blank ones. Lenders require complete documents for compliance, and missing pages can raise red flags or stall your application.

Think of it this way: It's easier to provide too much paperwork upfront than to go back and hunt for missing pieces later. So, when in doubt, send it all—it saves everyone time and keeps the process moving smoothly.

Story Time: Just the First Page

Let me tell you about Brian, a client who thought he had found a clever way to simplify his mortgage application process. When it came time to provide his bank statements, Brian sent over just the first page of each statement for the past year.

At first glance, everything seemed fine. Each first page showed a healthy balance, which Brian was clearly proud of. But as I started reviewing the documents, it was immediately obvious that something was missing.

I gave Brian a quick call.

"Hey, Brian," I said. "Thanks for sending over your bank statements, but I noticed you only sent the first pages. We'll need the full statements—all pages, including the transaction details."

There was a brief pause before Brian replied, half-jokingly, "Do you really need to see all my Starbucks visits? Because trust me, there are a lot of them!"

I laughed and reassured him, "We're not here to judge your caffeine habit, Brian. It's just that lenders require the full statements to comply with lending guidelines. We need to see all the transactions—not to pry, but to ensure there aren't any large or unusual deposits or withdrawals that need to be explained."

Brian sighed, clearly amused by the irony. "So, you're saying my great balance isn't enough?"

"Unfortunately, no," I said with a smile in my voice. "We need the whole story, not just the headline. It's all part of the process."

Brian promptly sent the remaining pages, and we were able to move forward smoothly. But his initial approach was a reminder of how important it is to provide complete documentation.

The Lesson

When it comes to bank statements, lenders need to see the full picture—all pages, not just the cover sheet. Even if you think the extra pages don't matter or show mundane details like your morning coffee routine, they're critical for compliance and transparency.

Remember: your mortgage expert isn't here to critique your spending habits. We just need to ensure everything checks out so your loan can be approved without delays. Save yourself—and us—the extra step, and send the full statements from the start.

Mistake #2: Large Deposits

Another reason we need all the pages of your bank statement is to track large deposits. These must be reviewed due to anti-money laundering laws. Even though you're probably not laundering money, the law requires us to verify the source of any large deposits.

Tip: If you have a lot of non-direct deposit funds coming into your account, consider stopping those transactions for 60 days before applying for a mortgage. Alternatively, open a new account or move your direct deposit to an account where only regular transactions occur.

Joint Statements: If all your accounts are at the same bank, they might be printed on joint statements. Keep this in mind when deciding where to keep your down payment and other major assets.

Mistake #3: Providing Screenshots Instead of Documents

A lot of people think they can just take a quick screenshot of their bank balance or pay stub and upload it. While screenshots can work in some cases, they often don't include all the necessary information, like your name or the last four digits of your Social Security number.

Story Time: The Screenshot Disaster

Let me tell you about Ryan, a tech-savvy client who thought he had streamlined the mortgage process by using his phone to upload documents. Instead of downloading PDFs or scanning physical copies, Ryan opted to take screenshots of everything—bank statements, pay stubs, tax forms, you name it.

When his files came in, it quickly became clear that we had a problem.

Some screenshots cut off key information, like account numbers or transaction dates. Others were blurry or missing entire pages. One bank statement was snapped with the phone's flash on, creating a glare that made it completely unreadable. While Ryan's intentions were good, the result was a digital jigsaw puzzle—and we couldn't move forward until we had clear, complete documents.

I called Ryan to explain the situation.

"Hey, Ryan," I started. "Thanks for sending everything over, but we need to talk about your screenshots."

"Is something wrong?" he asked, sounding genuinely puzzled.

"Well," I replied, "most of them are incomplete. Some pages are missing, and others are hard to read. Unfortunately, we'll need you to redo everything and provide the full documents."

The groan on the other end of the line was unmistakable. "You're kidding me," he said. "I thought I was saving time by snapping photos!"

"I get it," I reassured him. "Screenshots can work in certain cases, but only if they include all the necessary information and are clear and legible. In this case, it's better to download the full documents or scan them to make sure we don't miss anything."

Ryan reluctantly went back to the drawing board, this time taking the extra steps to provide complete, high-quality files. It was a frustrating detour for him, and I felt terrible delivering the bad news, but it was a valuable lesson in how technology, while convenient, isn't always the best solution.

The Lesson

Screenshots can sometimes work for submitting documents, but only if they're complete, clear, and include all identifying information. Whenever possible, download the full document directly from the source or scan a physical copy.

Taking the extra time upfront to ensure your documents are complete and legible can save you from headaches and delays later. Remember: your mortgage expert is here to help, but we can only work with what you provide. The clearer and more thorough your files, the smoother the process will be.

Mistake #4: Blacking Out Information

Here's one that always cracks me up—customers blacking out sections of their documents. They do this to prevent identity theft, which I totally understand. But think about it: I've already collected a lot of sensitive information from you—your Social Security number, birth date, where you work, where you live, etc. If I really wanted to steal your identity, I'd already have what I need.

Why It's a Problem: We need to verify all the information. If you alter the documents, we'll ask you to resend them. Remember, mortgage experts undergo extensive background checks, licensing exams, and federal scrutiny. We're not going to steal your identity—it's not worth the risk to our careers.

Mistake #5: Non-Sufficient Funds (NSF)

NSFs appear on your bank statement when you overdraw your account. If this happens regularly, it can raise red flags.

Tip: If you've had NSFs, let your mortgage expert know. We often have solutions or workarounds, but it's better to be upfront. If you can avoid providing statements with NSFs, it will make the process smoother.

Mistake #6: Not Providing All Documents

This one is simple but happens more often than you'd think. Sometimes, people believe we don't really need certain documents, so they don't bother providing them. I promise you, if we're asking for a document, it's because we need it.

Why We Ask: The guidelines and rules we follow are there for a reason, even if they seem excessive. We're not asking for documents out of curiosity—we're doing it to get you approved. So, save yourself and us the back-and-forth, and do your best to provide what we ask for.

Chapter 4: Pre-Qualification vs. Pre-Approval: What's the Difference?

You've likely heard of both pre-qualification and pre-approval, but the differences can be confusing. What's the difference, anyway? Surprisingly, there isn't always a significant difference, but let's break it down.

What's the Real Difference?

Every mortgage company defines these terms a little differently. Ideally, **pre-qualification** and **pre-approval** should mean different things, but sometimes they're used interchangeably.

- **Pre-Qualification:** Typically means that you've provided some basic information—like income, debts, and assets—but it hasn't been thoroughly vetted. It's more of an initial estimate.
- **Pre-Approval:** This should mean that your information has gone through an underwriting process—whether automated or manual—and you're approved to borrow up to a certain amount, assuming all the details you provided are accurate.

The key takeaway is that you want to ensure whoever you're working with has actually reviewed your application thoroughly. This means submitting all your documents, running your credit, and verifying your income and assets. Otherwise, you might find yourself in a sticky situation later on.

Story Time: The Push-Button Mortgage That Wasn't

Let me tell you about a client who learned the hard way that not all pre-approval letters are created equal. It started with a major lender—one I won't name—offering an online mortgage service. The process seemed almost too good to be true: you go online, fill out the necessary information, and the system automatically pulls your credit. Then, an automated underwriting system reviews your data and instantly generates an approval letter.

For many clients, this "push button, get mortgage" approach feels like the dream—fast, easy, and hassle-free. In theory, if the information entered by the client and the data on the credit report are accurate, it should work perfectly.

But for one client, it didn't.

Excited by the simplicity of the process, they filled out their information, received a glowing approval letter, and quickly got under contract for their dream home. Everything seemed to be falling into place, and they were thrilled—until reality set in.

When it came time to submit the supporting documents that a diligent mortgage expert would have asked for upfront, two major issues came to light:

1. **Inconsistent Income:** The client had reported a very large bonus they received that year as part of their regular income. While the bonus was indeed impressive, it wasn't consistent. Mortgage guidelines require income to be steady and predictable to count toward qualification. Unfortunately, the automated system didn't flag this issue. Once their documents were reviewed, the bonus was disqualified, leaving the client with far less qualifying income than they had counted on.

2. **Unreported Debt:** The client also owned a rental property, but the mortgage tied to that property didn't appear on their credit report. This happens occasionally with smaller lenders who don't report to all three credit bureaus. Because the automated system didn't account for this significant debt, the client's debt-to-income ratio (DTI) was drastically understated.

Suddenly, the approval letter that had given them so much confidence was essentially worthless. They were under contract for a home they couldn't afford based on their true financial profile, and the stress was palpable.

In a panic, they reached out to my team, desperate for help. We were able to step in and salvage the situation, but it wasn't easy. It required creative problem-solving, a mountain of additional paperwork, and a lot of back-and-forth with the seller to avoid losing the house. In the end, we got them to the finish line, but the process was far more stressful and complicated than it needed to be.

The Lesson

Not all pre-approval letters are created equal. While automated systems might seem convenient, they often lack the nuance and expertise required to ensure everything checks out. Buying a home is likely the largest financial transaction you'll ever make, and it deserves more than a "push-button" approach.

When you work with an experienced mortgage expert, we take the time to review your income, debts, and overall financial profile upfront, identifying potential issues before you're under contract. It might take a little longer, but the peace of mind—and the smoother process—are well worth it.

So, the next time you see an online ad promising instant mortgage approval, remember this: faster isn't always better. A thorough, personalized approach ensures you can move forward with confidence, knowing there won't be any surprises down the road.

Many people mistakenly focus solely on the interest rate they're being offered, without considering the reliability of the approval process itself. They might not realize that the approval letter they've received could be based on inaccurate or incomplete information. They go under contract, pay for inspections, and invest in other necessary steps, only to find out later that their approval isn't as solid as they thought.

While sometimes things do work out, and the initial approval turns out to be valid, I've seen too many deals fall apart because the letter was based on flawed or incomplete data. In my career, I've had to step in and save deals that were on the brink of collapse because the initial approval came from a company or individual who didn't fully understand the complexities of mortgage approval.

If you're reading this and taking the time to educate yourself about the mortgage process, you're already on the right track. But remember, it's crucial to ensure that the approval you're relying on is backed by a thorough review of your financial situation. This way, when you find your dream home, you can move forward with confidence, knowing that your offer is as strong as the paper it's written on.

We've discussed why it's so important for your pre-approval letter to hold weight, and here's why: many savvy realtors won't accept just any pre-approval letter. If they see letters from certain big banks or companies known for cutting corners—like not verifying paperwork or not checking credit thoroughly—they may advise the seller against accepting your offer. While the final decision is up to the seller, having a questionable pre-approval letter can seriously weaken your position in negotiations, especially in competitive markets where multiple offers are common.

You want your offer to be as strong as cash, and that's where a solid pre-approval letter comes into play. It shows the seller that you're a serious buyer with the financial backing to close the deal. Let me illustrate this with a story.

We had a client who found their dream home and quickly submitted an offer, only to be told by the realtor that their pre-approval letter wasn't good enough. The letter was from a large institution with a reputation for not thoroughly vetting clients, which made the seller's agent skeptical. They recommended the client get pre-approved by a more reputable lender, and that's when they came to us.

Understanding the urgency, we got to work immediately. Typically, the process takes about 24-48 hours, but knowing the client's situation, we expedited everything and had them fully approved within 4-5 hours. This quick turnaround allowed them to submit a strong offer and secure the home, despite the last-minute scramble. They were fortunate that another offer didn't come in during that time, but it was a close call.

The lesson here is that just having a pre-approval letter isn't enough—it needs to be from a lender who has done their due diligence. Not all letters are created equal, and in competitive markets, the quality of your pre-approval letter can make or break your chances of landing your dream home.

How Long Does It Take to Get Pre-Qualified or Pre-Approved?

Once you've submitted all the necessary paperwork, you're probably wondering, "How long does it take to get that prequalification or preapproval letter?" The typical answer is 24 to 48 hours—yes, we do mean business hours. So, if you submit everything late on a Friday night, it might be the end of Saturday or even Sunday before a mortgage expert can get it done. Keep in mind that many professionals don't work every single Saturday or Sunday, or they do so on an as-needed basis. It's not always reasonable to expect every mortgage expert to turn your file around within 24 to 48 hours especially when there is a weekend in the mix, but that timeframe is the average.

What If You're Self-Employed?

If you're self-employed, the process can take a little longer. We often need to dig deeper into your finances, which might involve running additional verifications or obtaining more documentation. This is why I highly encourage starting the process sooner rather than later. If it takes us 3 to 4 days to gather and review all the necessary paperwork, you want to ensure that we have the time to do it thoroughly. Rushing through this can lead to missed details, which might affect your ability to qualify for the loan.

Need It Sooner?

If you're in a situation where you need the prequalification or preapproval letter a bit sooner—say, you submit everything on a Thursday night but want to look at houses that weekend—let your mortgage expert know. Often, if they're able, they'll try to speed up the process for you. However, it's crucial not to rush things too much. You don't want important details to be overlooked simply because the process was hurried. Making financial decisions based on incomplete or rushed work can lead to complications down the line.

Why the Wait is Worth It

Taking the time to do things right is important. When we tell you that you're good to go, we want to be absolutely sure that you're truly in a position to make an offer on a property. This diligence helps ensure that when you're ready to buy that house, everything is in place and there won't be any last-minute surprises. So while waiting for a day or two might feel frustrating, it's a necessary part of ensuring that your financial foundation is solid before you take the next big step in buying a home.

What You Can Afford vs. What You Should Afford

Once we've gone through the initial steps of the mortgage process, we're going to let you know how much you can actually qualify for. At the start, you may have had an idea of what you want to qualify for—perhaps you envisioned a certain house value or price range—but this is the point where we get down to what you can truly afford.

Hard Pull vs. Soft Pull Credit Checks

To figure out what you qualify for, we'll need to pull your credit. You may have heard terms like "hard pull" and "soft pull" when it comes to credit checks, and you might be wondering what the difference is.

- **Hard Pull:** This is a more thorough check that can potentially impact your credit score. When we do a hard pull, credit agencies recognize that you're looking to make a major purchase, like buying a house. If you have too many hard pulls within a certain period, it can cause your credit score to drop slightly to significantly depending on how many pulls you have had. This is because multiple inquiries can signal to lenders that you're taking on more debt, which might make you a higher risk.
- **Soft Pull:** A soft pull is less invasive and does not affect your credit score. Think of it as a peek at your credit. We often do soft pulls during the prequalification or preapproval phase to get a snapshot of your credit. However, to fully qualify you for a mortgage, we will need to do a hard pull eventually.

So, once we've pulled your credit, we'll take a look at it and use that information to review your debts and other financial details. This is how we determine exactly how much you qualify for.

Finding Your Comfort Zone

After assessing your finances, we'll show you roughly what your mortgage payments might look like and how much house you can afford. But here's an important point: just because you can qualify for a certain amount doesn't necessarily mean you should take on that much debt.

For example, while you might be eligible for a loan that allows you to buy a bigger or more expensive home. In the end, the mortgage process is not just about what you qualify for—it's about what you can comfortably afford and what aligns with your financial goals. Whether you're applying solo or as a couple, a good mortgage expert will help you navigate these decisions, ensuring that the loan you get is the best fit for your situation.

Story Time: The Credit Score Dilemma

Let me introduce you to Lisa and Dan, a couple bursting with excitement as they prepared to buy their first home together. Both had successful careers and were eager to make their dream of homeownership a reality. But as we dove into the mortgage process, they hit an unexpected hurdle: their credit scores.

Lisa had excellent credit, the kind that unlocks the best interest rates and most favorable loan terms. Dan, however, wasn't in the same boat. Old collections had knocked his credit score down into the low 600s—a far cry from Lisa's stellar standing.

Credit scores play a crucial role in determining mortgage interest rates, and for Lisa and Dan, this posed a significant challenge. Mortgage lenders typically consider the lowest middle credit score of all applicants, meaning Dan's score would dictate their loan terms. Using his credit score would have resulted in a much higher interest rate, adding thousands to their overall payments and making the loan far more expensive than they had planned.

Instead of letting Dan's credit score hold them back, we proposed a creative solution: qualifying for the mortgage using only Lisa's income and credit score. By doing so, we were able to secure a much better interest rate and avoid the added costs associated with Dan's lower credit.

However, this approach came with a trade-off. Because the loan was based solely on Lisa's financial profile, she needed to qualify for the entire loan amount on her own. The lender treated it as if Lisa would be making all the mortgage payments herself, even though both spouses planned to contribute. It was a challenge, but Lisa's strong credit and solid income allowed her to meet the requirements.

With Lisa qualifying for the mortgage on her own, the couple closed on their dream home. But they didn't stop there. Once settled, Dan began working diligently to improve his credit score, paying down old debts and building a positive credit history.

After about a year, his credit score had significantly improved, and the couple decided it was time to refinance their mortgage. During the refinancing process, we added Dan to the loan, allowing both spouses to share financial responsibility and ownership. The new loan reflected the progress they had made together as a team.

The Lesson

This story shows that even if one spouse has a less-than-perfect credit score, there are creative ways to navigate the mortgage process and achieve homeownership. In Lisa and Dan's case, qualifying with only one spouse's credit and income allowed them to secure a better interest rate, avoiding the higher costs associated with a lower score.

Just because someone isn't on the loan at the start doesn't mean they can't join later. Strategies like refinancing can help couples adjust financial responsibilities once the timing is right.

The key takeaway? Be honest and upfront about your financial situation with your mortgage expert. With the right guidance and a little strategic planning, you can find solutions tailored to your circumstances. Whether it's qualifying with one person's income or creating a plan to improve credit over time, there's almost always a path to homeownership.

Chapter 5: Understanding Title vs. Loan: Who Really Owns the Property?

When it comes to owning a home, there are two critical concepts you need to understand: the **title** and the **loan**. These terms often confuse homebuyers, but they're crucial in determining ownership and responsibility for the mortgage.

What is the Title?

The title is a legal document that shows who owns the property. When your name is on the title, it means you have ownership rights to the property. This is true regardless of whether or not your name is on the mortgage loan.

What is the Loan?

The loan (or mortgage) is the financial agreement between you and the lender. It outlines the terms of repayment for the money you borrowed to purchase the home. If your name is on the loan, you're legally responsible for repaying the mortgage.

Can You Be on the Title Without Being on the Loan?

Yes, you can be on the title without being on the loan. This means you can own the property and have legal rights to it without being financially responsible for the mortgage. Here's how it works:

- **On the Title, Not on the Loan**: If you're on the title but not on the loan, you legally own part of the property, but you're not responsible for repaying the mortgage. For example, if a couple buys a home, one partner might be on the loan due to having better credit, but both might be on the title to share ownership.

- **On the Loan, Not on the Title**: This scenario is rare but possible. For instance, someone might co-sign a mortgage to help another person qualify for a loan but not want any ownership stake in the property. In this case, they're financially responsible for the loan but have no ownership rights. This usually happens when a parent helps a child buy a home.

Who Should Be on the Title?

You can technically add anyone you want to the title of your property. However, adding someone to the title means they legally own a portion of the property, which can have implications for taxes, inheritance, and legal responsibilities.

A Word of Caution

While it's legally possible to add anyone to the title, it's usually best to be cautious. Adding someone to your title means they have ownership rights, which can complicate matters if your relationship changes or if there are legal disputes.

For example, adding a friend or distant relative to the title because they co-signed the loan might lead to issues later on, especially if you want to sell the property or if there are disagreements about the property's use. It's always wise to consult with a legal professional or title company representative before making any decisions about the title.

Summary

- **Title**: Determines who owns the property.
- **Loan**: Determines who is responsible for repaying the mortgage.
- **Title without Loan**: You can own the property without being responsible for the mortgage.
- **Loan without Title**: You can be responsible for the mortgage without owning the property (rare but possible).

Understanding the difference between the title and the loan ensures you make informed decisions about property ownership and financial responsibility. If you have any doubts, it's always a good idea to seek expert advice to avoid complications down the road.

Estimating Your Monthly Payment

When you're buying a home, it's natural to want to know exactly what your monthly mortgage payment will be. However, unlike buying a car, where the payment is straightforward and predictable, a mortgage payment has a bit more complexity. When we provide you with a pre-approval, we give you a ballpark estimate of your monthly payment. However, it's important to understand that this is an estimate, not an exact number. There are several factors that can affect your final payment, and it's crucial to be aware of them:

- **Down Payment:** The amount you decide to put down on your home will significantly impact your monthly mortgage payment. If you increase your down payment, your loan amount decreases, resulting in a lower monthly payment. Conversely, if you choose to put less money down, your loan amount—and therefore your monthly payment—will be higher. This is a factor you control, but it can change as you decide how much to allocate for your down payment.
- **Homeowners Insurance:** Insurance rates vary based on several factors, including the age and condition of the home, its location, and the number of insurance claims

previously made on the property, as well as the number of claims you, yourself, may have had previously.

- **Property Taxes:** Taxes can vary significantly depending on the area, and they directly impact your payment. Property taxes are set by local governments and can increase over time. This increase can be reflected in your monthly mortgage payment if your taxes go up depending on if you have your property taxes escrowed.

Story Time: The Case of the Older Home vs. New Build

Meet Rachel, a client who was wrestling with a tough decision during her home-buying journey. She had narrowed her options down to two vastly different properties. One was a charming older home, full of character, built in the 1950s. The other was a sleek, modern new build completed just six months earlier. Surprisingly, the price tags on both homes were almost identical, making her choice even harder.

What tipped the scales, though, wasn't charm or modern conveniences—it was the hidden cost of homeowners insurance.

Rachel assumed that since the homes were priced the same, their insurance costs would be similar too. But the reality was quite different. Older homes often have components that are closer to the end of their lifespan and more likely to need repairs or replacement. Things like plumbing, electrical systems, and especially the roof can drive up insurance costs significantly.

In Texas, where hailstorms are a common occurrence, the age of the roof matters a lot. The older home had an aging roof that would likely need repairs sooner rather than later, while the new build had a brand-new roof with higher resistance to storm damage.

Another factor that worked against the older home was its claims history. This property had multiple past insurance claims, which drove up its premiums. On the other hand, the new build had no claims history and all-new systems, resulting in a much lower insurance cost.

Despite the higher premiums, Rachel's heart was set on the older home. She loved its charm and character, and it felt like the perfect place to call home. But this choice came with a financial trade-off: the higher insurance premium added about $150 to her monthly mortgage payment. While Rachel was comfortable with this decision, it's a cost that adds up over time, making the home more expensive to own in the long run.

The Lesson

Rachel's experience highlights how even small details—like the age of a home or its claims history—can have a big impact on your overall costs. Homeowners insurance premiums can vary widely, ranging from an extra $15-$20 per month to $200-$300 or more, depending on factors like a home's age, location, and claims history.

When you're buying a home, it's essential to look beyond the sticker price. Consider things like insurance costs, maintenance, and potential repairs. These hidden expenses can significantly affect your budget and the true cost of homeownership.

By understanding these factors and working closely with your mortgage expert, you can make an informed decision that aligns with your financial goals.

Story Time: The Property Tax Confusion

Let me tell you about Tom, a long-time homeowner who gave me one of the most memorable calls of my career. Back when I worked in a call center for the largest mortgage institution in the country—right before the 2008 crash—I received a call that started with a bang.

As soon as I answered, Tom launched into a tirade, cursing up a storm. He was livid, and I could barely get a word in as he ranted for a solid ten minutes. His anger was focused, and from what little I could gather, he believed we had pulled a fast one on him.

When he finally paused for breath, I calmly said, "Tom, let me make sure I understand your concern." From his perspective, we had illegally raised his interest rate and increased his monthly mortgage payment without his permission. He was convinced we had done something underhanded, and he wanted answers.

After verifying his identity, I pulled up his account to take a closer look. Sure enough, his interest rate and principal payment hadn't changed a bit. The real culprit? An increase in his property taxes. Since Tom's taxes were paid through an escrow account attached to his mortgage, the monthly payment had gone up to cover the higher tax bill.

When I explained this to him, he paused before asking a question that still makes me laugh: "Why did you let them do that?"

I couldn't help but chuckle as I clarified, "Tom, property taxes are set by your local government, not your mortgage company. We don't have any control over them. If you're unhappy with the increase, you'll need to contact your local tax authority to discuss it."

After a moment of silence, he sighed. "Well, that makes more sense. Thanks for clearing it up."

It was a classic case of misunderstanding how property taxes work, and to be fair, it's something many homeowners don't fully grasp.

The Lesson

Tom's story highlights the importance of understanding all the elements that make up your mortgage payment. While your lender is responsible for collecting and managing your escrow payments, if you have one, property taxes are determined by your local government. Any changes in your taxes—whether due to reassessments, bond measures, or new local fees—can directly affect your monthly payment.

If you notice an increase, check your escrow statement and contact your local tax authority for clarification or to file an appeal. Remember, your mortgage company is simply the middleman—they have no say in how much you're charged.

By understanding how taxes impact your payment, you'll avoid surprises and know exactly where to direct your questions.

What is PMI?

PMI is a type of insurance that protects the lender if you default on your loan. It's typically required if you're putting down less than 20% of the home's purchase price. This requirement is actually where the misconception about needing 20% down originates. Before PMI existed, buyers did need to put down 20% to secure a mortgage. PMI was introduced to reduce the lender's risk, allowing buyers to put down less than 20% while still being able to get a mortgage.

When Do You Need PMI?

If you're not putting down 20% and you're not using a special loan program like a VA loan (which is available to veterans, active duty service members, and some reservists), you'll likely need to pay for PMI.

- **FHA Loans:** With FHA loans, PMI is a fixed amount regardless of your credit score, debt-to-income ratio, or other factors. Everyone pays the same rate.
- **Conventional Loans:** PMI on conventional loans varies. The amount you pay is influenced by factors like your credit score, the amount of debt you have compared to your income, and the term of the loan. Because of this, PMI can be higher or lower depending on your financial situation.

How Does PMI Affect Your Payment?

By the time you receive your pre-qualification or pre-approval letter, we'll have likely discussed which loan program you'll be using, so you should have a rough idea of how much PMI will add to your monthly payment. However, it's crucial to remember that other components of your payment, like homeowners insurance and property taxes, might not be fully determined at that stage.

Now that we've covered most of the key factors influencing your mortgage payment, let's talk about the final major component: principal and interest. This part of your payment is determined by the length of time you want to take to repay the loan. The most common term is 30 years, especially for first-time homebuyers. However, there are other options, like 15-year, 20-year, and even 10-year loan terms. Most people stick with the 30-year option because it keeps monthly payments more manageable.

Principal and Interest

When you receive your pre-qualification or pre-approval letter, we'll likely have a clear idea of your loan term, so you'll have a good sense of your principal and interest payment. For example, if your loan amount is $X, your principal and interest payments will be roughly $Y. However, it's important to remember that this amount can be affected by interest rates.

Understanding Interest Rates

Interest rates play a huge role in determining your monthly payment. But here's the tricky part: you typically cannot lock in an interest rate until you're under contract to buy a specific property. This is because interest rates are tied to the property you're purchasing. Here's a quick story to illustrate:

Story Time: The Broken Rate Lock

Meet Jake, a first-time homebuyer who was ecstatic to go under contract on a home that checked all the boxes on his wish list. As part of the process, we locked in an interest rate for him, ensuring his mortgage terms would stay stable. Jake was excited, thinking everything was falling into place—but then came the home inspection.

The inspection revealed some significant issues: an aging roof, outdated electrical wiring, and a leaking water heater. The repair costs were too high, and the sellers weren't willing to negotiate. After careful consideration, Jake made the tough decision to walk away from the property. It was the right move for his financial health, but it introduced a new challenge: the rate lock.

Rate locks are tied to specific properties. When Jake walked away from the first home, the original rate lock had to be broken. When he found a new property and went under contract, we secured a new rate lock. Fortunately for Jake, the timing worked in his favor—interest rates had dipped, and we were able to lock in an even better rate for the second property.

But this isn't always the case. Interest rates can fluctuate based on market conditions and economic trends, which are outside anyone's control. If rates had risen, Jake could have faced higher monthly payments than he originally anticipated.

The Lesson

Jake's experience highlights how rate locks work and why flexibility is key during the home-buying process. While rate locks provide stability, they're tied to specific properties. If you need to walk away from a home for any reason, a new rate lock will be required for your next property, and the terms may not always be as favorable.

It's also a reminder that buying a home involves many moving parts—far more than a typical car purchase, where payment terms are fixed early on. Rate fluctuations, property-specific contingencies, and inspection results are just a few of the variables that can impact your final costs.

Working closely with your mortgage expert ensures you're prepared for these challenges. With the right guidance, you can confidently navigate the process and make informed decisions every step of the way—just like Jake did.

Estimating Your Payment

To help you get a better idea of your potential payment, we usually start by asking if you have a specific area in mind where you'd like to buy. If you do, we can look up the approximate property taxes and average home prices in that area to give you a rough estimate of your payment. If you're unsure where you'll buy, we'll use worst-case scenarios, like the highest possible property taxes, to ensure you still qualify. This way, if you end up in a lower-tax area, you might have more buying power.

Why Local Expertise Matters

Working with a mortgage expert who knows the local laws and market conditions is crucial. Each state has its own unique regulations that can significantly impact the cost, loan programs, and even the final payment. For instance, Texas has distinct home equity laws and varying property tax rates, New York has tax stamps, Florida imposes an intangible tax, and several states follow community property rules. These differences can complicate the mortgage process if your lender isn't familiar with them.

If you're working with someone out of state or not familiar with these nuances, it can lead to costly mistakes. This is why it's essential to choose a mortgage expert who has local knowledge or significant experience in the state where you're buying. They can help you navigate these complexities and avoid potential pitfalls.

Story Time: The Texas Tax Trap

Let me tell you about James and Sarah, a couple who nearly lost their dream home because their lender didn't understand the complexities of Texas property taxes.

James and Sarah were working with an out-of-state lender who seemed knowledgeable at first glance. Everything appeared to be going smoothly—until the lender underestimated their property taxes.

Here's the issue: Texas has unique tax structures, and not all taxes are visible on the county website. For example, if you're buying a home in Frisco, Texas, and it's located in Denton County, you'll pay county taxes to Denton. But your school taxes might go to Collin County, where most of Frisco is located. This dual-county setup can easily trip up anyone unfamiliar with Texas tax laws.

In James and Sarah's case, the out-of-state lender missed this nuance and significantly underestimated their taxes. When the accurate tax amounts came in, it turned out they no longer qualified for the loan.

The couple was devastated. They had already spent money on inspections, earnest money, and option money, all of which were at risk of being lost. Scrambling to save the deal, they came to us for help.

Fortunately, we were able to step in, account for the correct tax amounts, and restructure their loan to get them qualified. But it was a stressful and unnecessary ordeal that could have been avoided with a lender who truly understood Texas's unique tax system.

The Lesson

James and Sarah's experience highlights how critical it is to work with a mortgage expert who understands local laws and regulations. Different states have different rules, and even small oversights can create significant problems during the home-buying process.

Even though our team handles loans in multiple states, we always take the time to understand the local nuances of each area. If you're buying in a state with complex rules—like Texas—verify that your lender has the expertise to navigate them. It could save you from a costly and stressful situation.

The Importance of Accurate Pre-Approval

The primary goal of your pre-approval letter is to give you a clear ballpark figure of what you can afford and ensure that the payment is something you're comfortable with. Just because you qualify for a certain amount doesn't necessarily mean you should spend that much. Often, you might qualify for more than you're comfortable paying, so it's essential to consider what you can realistically afford.

It's also vital to be aware of factors that can change your buying power, such as fluctuations in interest rates or significant changes in your financial situation. If anything major changes, you need to communicate with your mortgage expert immediately. They can guide you through how these changes might impact your loan, advising you on the best course of action.

A good mortgage expert won't just say "no" if you're facing challenges. Instead, they'll help you understand the implications of your decisions and work with you to find solutions that align with your financial goals. Open communication is key—you and your mortgage expert should be on the same page throughout the entire process.

Story Time: Why You Should Discuss Major Financial Changes with Your Mortgage Expert

Let me tell you about Jessica and Mark, a couple who were just days away from closing on their dream home. Everything seemed to be in order, and the finish line was in sight. Then, on the Monday before their scheduled Friday closing, Jessica called me with a question.

"We're at the home improvement store," she said. "They're offering a 0% interest credit card. Can I use it to buy a fridge?"

I appreciated her asking first. I explained that while she technically could, opening a new line of credit before closing would require additional paperwork, which could potentially delay their loan closing. I suggested waiting until after the closing to avoid any complications. Jessica agreed, and I thought we were all set.

The real twist came a few days later.

On Thursday, I got a call from my processor about an issue with the final Verification of Employment (VOE). As part of the loan process, we contact the borrower's employer within 48 hours of closing to confirm they're still employed. This time, there was a problem: Mark—the sole income earner on the loan—was no longer employed at the company we had verified.

I immediately called Jessica and Mark to find out what was going on. "Did you quit, get fired, or find a new job?" I asked.

Mark, thankfully, had already started a new job, but this change threw a wrench into the process. Verifying the new employment meant gathering additional paperwork and approvals—steps that could potentially delay their Friday closing.

Jessica was understandably upset. "We have movers scheduled, and we can't afford a delay!" she said.

I empathized but reminded her that the job change was something we needed to know about as soon as it happened. Jessica admitted they didn't think it would matter. Thankfully, my team worked efficiently, and with the couple's cooperation, we managed to gather the necessary documents in record time. By the end of the day, everything was back on track, and they closed as scheduled.

The Lesson

Jessica and Mark's experience underscores why it's critical to keep your mortgage expert informed about any major financial changes—whether it's making a large purchase, changing jobs, or opening a new line of credit.

Even seemingly small decisions can impact your loan approval or delay your closing. Once your loan closes, you're free to make those changes, but until then, transparency is key. Communicating with your mortgage expert helps you avoid unnecessary stress, last-minute crises, and potential delays in closing on your home.

When in doubt, ask. We're here to guide you through the process and ensure everything goes as smoothly as possible.

Chapter 6: Understanding Loan Types, Terms, and Down Payments

When you're going through the mortgage process, it's crucial to understand how different loan types, terms, and down payment amounts can affect what you qualify for and ultimately, what you can afford. Each of these factors plays a significant role in determining your eligibility and the conditions of your loan.

Loan Types

There are several types of loans, each with its own guidelines and stipulations. These guidelines determine how much you can borrow, the interest rates you'll be offered, and other critical factors. The main categories of loans are:

1. **Government Loans**: This includes VA loans, FHA loans, and USDA loans. Each of these has specific requirements and benefits. For example, VA loans are for veterans and typically require no down payment, while FHA loans are popular for first-time homebuyers because of their lower credit score requirements.

2. **Conventional Loans**: These are loans not insured by the government and are typically set by Fannie Mae and

Freddie Mac guidelines. The loan limits are determined annually and can vary by state or county.

3. **Non-Conforming Loans**: These include jumbo loans, which exceed the conforming loan limits set by Fannie Mae and Freddie Mac. They also include non-QM (non-qualified mortgage) loans, which are designed for borrowers with unique circumstances, such as those who are self-employed or have irregular income.

Loan Terms

Loan terms refer to the length of time you have to repay your loan. The most common loan terms are:

- **30-Year Term**: The most popular option, providing the lowest monthly payment.
- **20-Year Term**: Offers a balance between a lower interest rate and a higher monthly payment.
- **15-Year Term**: Allows you to pay off your loan faster, with higher monthly payments but lower overall interest costs.
- **10-Year Term**: The highest monthly payments but the least amount of interest paid over the life of the loan.

Choosing the right loan term depends on your financial goals and how much you're comfortable paying each month.

Down Payments

Your down payment is the amount of money you pay upfront when purchasing a home. The amount of your down payment can vary greatly depending on the type of loan you choose:

- **0% Down**: Available with VA and USDA loans, though you may still need to cover closing costs unless someone else, such as the seller, covers them.
- **3%-5% Down**: Typical for conventional and FHA loans (for FHA it's 3.5% and in rare cases, a conventional loan can be as low as 3%)
- **10%-20% Down**: Required for non-conforming loans. To avoid paying PMI (private mortgage insurance) on conventional loans, you will be required to put down 20%.

It's important to note that even if your loan requires no down payment, such as with a VA loan, that doesn't mean you won't have other upfront costs like closing costs. A common misconception is that "0% down" means you don't have to bring any money to the closing table, which isn't typically the case unless other arrangements are made.

The Importance of Expert Guidance

With so many loan options and variations, it's easy to see why working with an experienced mortgage expert is essential. There are countless combinations of loan types, terms, and down payment scenarios, and you need an expert who can help you navigate these complexities and find the best fit for your unique situation.

Story Time: Down Payment Misconceptions

Meet Lisa, a client who was hesitant to even start the mortgage process. She had always dreamed of owning a home but was convinced she wouldn't qualify. When we finally spoke, her worries became clear: Lisa believed she needed a 740 credit score and a 20% down payment to get approved for a mortgage.

As we talked, I asked her a few questions about her financial situation. To her surprise, we discovered that she had an excellent credit score and had saved more than enough money to buy a home. For her particular loan program, only a 3% down payment was required.

Lisa was thrilled to learn she didn't need to wait years to save up 20% or put her dreams on hold. With her qualifications, she was able to buy a home sooner than she ever expected.

The Lesson

Lisa's story highlights a common misconception about down payments. Many people assume they need 20% down or perfect credit to qualify for a mortgage, but that's rarely the case.

There are loan programs available with much lower down payment requirements—sometimes as low as 3%—and options tailored to different financial situations.

The key takeaway? Don't let assumptions hold you back. Speak with a mortgage expert who can evaluate your situation, guide you through the options, and help you find solutions that fit your needs. Homeownership might be closer than you think!

Now that we've covered the essentials of prequalification, preapproval, loan types, terms, and down payments, you should have a good understanding of what to expect in the early stages of your home-buying journey. Now, we'll dive into the next steps in the process, helping you move closer to securing your dream home.

Chapter 7: Locating a Real Estate Expert

Finding the right real estate expert is a crucial first step in your home-buying journey. A knowledgeable and trustworthy agent will guide you through the complexities of the market, help you find the best properties, and negotiate deals that fit your needs. Let's explore how to identify the right real estate professional and what to consider when preparing to search for your ideal home.

Should You Pick a Real Estate Expert First?

Now, you might be thinking, "Well, I already picked a real estate expert before getting pre-approved." If that's the case, and maybe your real estate expert even connected you with a mortgage expert, you might be wondering if you need to go through this section at all. And that's okay—feel free to skip it if you've already aligned yourself with the right experts.

However, it's crucial to understand why getting pre-qualified or pre-approved before seriously searching for a home is such a key first step. Without knowing what you can afford, you could be wasting time looking at homes outside your budget or, worse, falling in love with a home only to find out later that you don't qualify for the loan amount needed to purchase it. To avoid these frustrations, **step one should always be to get pre-approved**. This process gives you a clear understanding of your financial situation and what homes you should realistically be looking at.

Of course, I understand the excitement that comes with house hunting. Many people jump right into the search and find an agent without thinking about financing first. If that's you, don't worry—it's not the end of the world! You've already got a real estate expert on your side, and that's a great start. But if you haven't chosen an agent yet, let's dive into how to select the best real estate professional for your needs.

How to Pick a Great Real Estate Agent

So, how do you pick one of these great agents? The key is finding someone who is **reputable** and **knowledgeable**, but that can sometimes be easier said than done. You may be wondering, "How do I know if they're reputable and knowledgeable?" Let's break it down because, honestly, **experience alone** is not always the best indicator. Some newer agents are incredibly sharp and committed, while there are agents who have been around for years and may lack up-to-date knowledge or have a less-than-stellar reputation.

Here are some practical ways to determine if an agent is the right fit for you:

1. Checking Their Reviews

The first step in selecting a great real estate agent is **checking their reviews**. Online reviews are a powerful tool to understand what others have experienced with that agent. It's important to look at both **good and bad reviews** to get a balanced perspective. Here's why:

- **Glowing reviews aren't always unbiased.** Some clients may have known the agent personally for years, making them more likely to overlook any flaws and sing their praises no matter what. So, while positive reviews are important, be mindful that some may not be entirely objective.
- **Negative reviews may not tell the whole story.** On the flip side, there are clients who, no matter how hard the agent worked, just couldn't be satisfied. Whether it was due to factors outside the agent's control—like issues with a property inspection or a last-minute hiccup in financing—some clients may unfairly hold the agent responsible for everything.

When reading reviews, keep both perspectives in mind and look for **patterns** in the feedback. If an agent consistently gets high marks for responsiveness, market knowledge, and negotiation skills, that's a good sign. If the complaints are more about things outside their control, like a bad appraisal, it may not be as much of a red flag.

Referrals Still Matter, But Do Your Own Research

If you've been referred to an agent by a friend or family member, that's a great start. Referrals usually hold a lot of weight because they come from people you trust. However, I always recommend doing a bit of digging on your own. Even with a personal referral, you want to be sure that the agent is the right fit for your specific needs.

- **Look them up online.** Check their presence on real estate platforms and social media. Are they active? Do they regularly update their listings and engage with their audience?
- **Verify their track record.** Look at their recent transactions and how long homes stay on the market. This gives you an idea of how effective they are in your area.

By taking a balanced approach—reading reviews carefully and verifying referrals—you'll ensure that the agent you choose is truly worth their reputation.

2. Check Their Knowledge of the Area

Another key factor to consider when choosing a real estate agent is how familiar they are with the specific area you're looking to buy in. Take Texas, for example—it's a massive state, and no agent will have intimate knowledge of every city or neighborhood. Most agents specialize in particular regions, and understanding what areas they cover is crucial to ensuring you're getting the right expert for your needs.

For instance, some agents may have experience in broad areas like **Dallas-Fort Worth (DFW)** or **Austin**, while others may focus solely on **Houston**. Then, it can get even more granular. You may find agents who specialize in just one specific city, like **Plano**, a northern suburb of DFW, rather than the entire metro area. This level of focus can be beneficial because these agents often have deep local knowledge about:

- **Neighborhood trends**
- **School districts**
- **Future developments**
- **Zoning laws**
- **Community amenities**

How to Find Out What Areas They Specialize In

To determine if an agent specializes in the area you're interested in, here are a few strategies:

- **Check their website:** Many agents list the areas they serve directly on their homepage or in their bio. They may also highlight recent transactions in those areas, which is a good indicator of their familiarity.

- **Look at reviews:** Clients often mention where they worked with the agent. If you're seeing consistent mentions of success in a specific city or neighborhood, that's a good sign the agent knows the area well.
- **Ask directly:** Sometimes, the easiest and most effective way to find out is to simply ask. Whether you reach out via email or phone, you can inquire specifically about their experience in the city or neighborhood you're interested in. A good agent will be happy to provide details and may even offer local insights on the spot.

Choosing an agent with **local expertise** is key to a smoother buying process, as they'll have the inside scoop on the area's housing market, trends, and potential future growth.

3. Know What You Want in an Agent

The second important consideration when choosing a real estate agent is understanding what **you** want. This involves taking a closer look at your personality, your preferred communication style, and how much involvement you expect from the agent throughout the process. Everyone's needs are different, and the perfect agent for someone else might not be the best fit for you.

Here are a few key questions to ask yourself (and anyone else you may be buying the home with):

- **Do you prefer a direct, take-charge approach?**
  Some people like an agent who takes the lead, constantly checks in and is always driving the process forward. If you prefer a lot of guidance and proactive communication, an assertive agent who follows up frequently could be a great fit.
- **Do you prefer a more laid-back, hands-off approach?**
  On the flip side, if you're someone who wants space to make decisions without feeling pressured, you might prefer an agent who gives you room to breathe. This type of agent may reach out occasionally but lets you take the lead on communication and decisions.
- **How much hand-holding do you want?**
  Some buyers appreciate having their agent walk them through every step of the process, offering frequent updates and checking in regularly. Others prefer less frequent touchpoints, only reaching out when necessary and giving them the freedom to ask questions when needed.

Understanding your preferred style will help you find the right agent, and it's something you should discuss upfront when interviewing potential candidates.

A Real-Life Example: Finding the Right Agent

Let me tell you about Emily and Jason, a couple who were excited to buy their first home but quickly realized how important it is to work with an agent whose style matches your own.

We initially paired Emily and Jason with Sarah, an agent who was one of the best in the business. Sarah was incredibly knowledgeable, highly experienced, and had a reputation for getting clients under contract quickly. She was proactive, always checking in, and kept the process moving at a fast pace. For many buyers, Sarah's take-charge approach was perfect.

But for Emily and Jason, it wasn't the right fit.

They were much more laid-back and preferred a slower, more relaxed process. While they appreciated Sarah's expertise, her frequent follow-ups and fast-moving style felt overwhelming to them. What Sarah intended as proactive guidance came across as pressure, leaving Emily and Jason feeling uncomfortable and stressed.

Eventually, they decided to switch to a different agent, Mark, whose approach was a better match for their needs. Mark was more laid-back, checking in occasionally without being overbearing. This change allowed Emily and Jason to feel more comfortable and in control of their home-buying experience, and they ultimately found a home they loved.

The Lesson

This story highlights how crucial it is to find an agent whose style aligns with your own preferences. A highly qualified agent is important, but so is working with someone who makes you feel comfortable during what can be a stressful process.

Whether you prefer a fast-paced, hands-on approach or a more relaxed and patient style, there's an agent out there who's a perfect match for you. Take the time to communicate your expectations upfront, and don't hesitate to switch if the fit doesn't feel right.

With the right agent by your side, the home-buying journey can be both smooth and enjoyable.

Know Yourself and Your Style

The takeaway here is simple: **know yourself, your personality, and what you want in an agent**. The more you understand your preferences, the easier it will be to choose someone whose style aligns with yours. Whether you prefer someone who's hands-on or someone who gives you space, the right agent will make the entire home-buying process more enjoyable and less stressful.

4. Consider the Agent's Professional Relationships

Another important factor when choosing a real estate agent is to look at the **professional relationships** they've built over time. The real estate world is highly collaborative, and the connections an agent has can be a valuable asset to you as a buyer. Strong relationships within the industry can offer an agent access to off-market deals, insider information, and more.

Here are a few reasons why an agent's relationships matter:

Access to Off-Market Deals

A well-connected agent may have access to properties that haven't yet hit the market. Agents with strong ties in the industry often hear about homes that are about to be listed and can give you an early advantage, especially in a competitive market. These relationships can help you find your dream home before it's even officially available.

Collaboration with Other Agents

Agents who have good working relationships with other real estate professionals are more likely to engage in **collaborative negotiations**. When agents know and trust each other, deals tend to go smoother. For example, if an agent has a good rapport with the listing agent on a property you're interested in, they may be able to communicate more effectively, helping to streamline negotiations and avoid unnecessary conflicts.

Access to Knowledge and Resources

The real estate market is constantly changing—new laws, regulations, and market trends pop up regularly. A great agent will have a network of resources they can lean on for insights and advice. These relationships can include:

- **Lenders** who can offer insight into mortgage trends and help you secure better financing terms or products.
- **Inspectors** who provide thorough evaluations to protect you from hidden issues.
- **Contractors** for renovations or repairs you may need during or after the home-buying process.

How to Evaluate Their Network

To assess whether an agent has strong industry relationships, consider the following:

- **Ask about their connections.** When you interview potential agents, ask them who they typically work with and how those relationships help their clients. Do they have reliable contacts for lenders, inspectors, or contractors?
- **Check their reputation within the community.** Agents with strong networks are often well-regarded in the local

real estate community. You can sometimes gauge this by talking to other professionals in the industry or by seeing if the agent is involved in local real estate groups or organizations.

- **See how proactive they are.** If an agent has built a solid network, they should be able to leverage it to your advantage. For instance, they might mention upcoming listings or special opportunities during your search, demonstrating how their connections benefit you.

By choosing an agent with strong relationships, you'll gain access to a wider range of resources, from market insights to off-market opportunities, ensuring you're in the best position to find and secure the perfect home.

5. Look for an Agent Who Will Challenge You

A great real estate agent doesn't just **listen** to what you want—they also know when to **push back** and challenge your thinking. A good agent isn't afraid to give constructive feedback, especially if they think your expectations are a bit unrealistic. This kind of pushback can be incredibly valuable because it helps you **set realistic expectations**, which is crucial to a smooth and successful home-buying process.

Why It's Important for an Agent to Challenge You

1. **Broadening Your Options** While it's important for an agent to listen to your needs, they also have a deeper understanding of the market and may suggest areas or property types you hadn't considered. For example, they might say, "I know you're focused on this neighborhood, but have you considered this nearby area? It has similar amenities and could be a better fit within your budget." A good agent uses their knowledge to expand your thinking and help you find options that might be better aligned with your needs, even if they weren't part of your initial search.

2. **Managing Expectations** Sometimes, buyers come into the market with expectations that may not match reality—whether it's the price point, the size of the home, or the specific neighborhood. A great agent will recognize when your expectations are off and gently push you to reconsider or make adjustments. For example, if your budget doesn't align with the features you're looking for, a skilled agent might say, "I understand you want a home with all of these features, but based on your budget, you may need to compromise in certain areas. Here's what's more realistic." **Expectation-setting** is key because it prevents disappointment down the line and helps keep the process moving efficiently.

3. **Balancing Wants and Needs** An experienced agent can help you distinguish between your "must-haves" and "nice-to-haves" in a property. They'll ask questions like, "Is having a large yard more important than being closer to the city center?" or "Would you consider a smaller home if it meant getting into the neighborhood you love?" This type of conversation helps clarify your priorities, ensuring you make the best decision for your lifestyle and budget.

4. **Realistic Market Insights** The real estate market can be competitive, and sometimes it moves faster than buyers expect. A knowledgeable agent might challenge you on timing or decision-making, encouraging you to act quickly when necessary. For example, if you hesitate too long on a home in a hot market, the agent may push you to make an offer before you lose the opportunity.

Expectation Setting Is Crucial

Setting expectations upfront is one of the most important aspects of working with a real estate agent. By doing this, your agent can ensure you're not wasting time looking at properties outside your price range or with features that are simply unavailable in your desired location. It also makes sure that when you do find the right home, you're prepared to move forward confidently, without second-guessing yourself.

A good agent will **listen to your needs** but also **challenge your assumptions** when necessary. This balance between guidance and advocacy makes the home-buying process more efficient, realistic, and ultimately, more satisfying.

By working with an agent who can both support and challenge you, you'll be better prepared to find a home that fits not just your wants, but your needs and long-term goals.

6. Trust Your Gut Feeling

Sometimes, choosing the right real estate agent comes down to something simple: **trusting your gut feeling**. You might be interviewing an agent who ticks all the boxes on paper, but if you don't feel a strong connection or confidence in them, it's perfectly okay to move on and keep looking. On the other hand, if an agent might not have all the perfect credentials but you feel they truly understand your needs, that gut feeling can be a strong indicator that they're the right choice for you.

Follow Your Instincts

If something feels off during the initial meetings or conversations with an agent, don't ignore that feeling. Buying a home is a significant financial and emotional decision, and you need to feel completely comfortable with the person who's guiding you through it. If an agent seems disinterested, unresponsive or just doesn't click with you, it's okay to keep looking for someone who does.

Your agent should be someone you trust and feel confident working with during what can sometimes be a stressful process.

On the other hand, if your instincts tell you that an agent is a great fit, even if they don't have the perfect resume or vast experience, trust that feeling too. A positive connection can make all the difference in the home-buying journey.

A Personal Story: Trusting My Gut

When my husband and I were searching for a new home, we found ourselves in an interesting dilemma. Being in the real estate industry, we had connections with so many amazing realtors, each of whom brought something unique to the table. Choosing just one felt almost impossible.

But something about one particular agent stood out to me.

We were looking for a home with more land, and this agent specialized in properties with land—a niche not every realtor is experienced in. My gut told me this was the right person for us, even though they weren't necessarily the "perfect fit" in every category. Still, they challenged us in all the right ways, asking questions we hadn't even thought to consider:

- "Have you considered the way the house is oriented on the land?"
- "What about the layout of the yard?"

- "Have you thought about the school district or potential future development in the area?"

Even with my background in real estate, these weren't factors I had fully considered. The agent's questions pushed our thinking and helped us prioritize what truly mattered in a home with land. Thanks to their expertise, we were able to approach the decision with a new perspective and make a choice we felt confident about.

The Lesson

Sometimes, the "perfect fit" isn't about finding someone who checks every box—it's about finding someone who challenges your thinking in the best ways.

Trusting your gut when choosing an agent can lead to a partnership that broadens your perspective and helps you make more informed decisions. Whether it's their experience in a specific niche or the way they ask the right questions, the right agent will guide you toward the home that truly fits your needs.

Don't Be Afraid of a Little Pushback

It's important to remember that an agent who **challenges you** isn't a bad thing—it's often a great thing. When a professional pushes back on your assumptions or encourages you to look at things from a different angle, it can broaden your perspective and help you make a smarter choice.

A home is one of the largest financial transactions you'll make, so having someone who stretches your thought process is invaluable. In the end, a little pushback may be exactly what you need to ensure you're making the right decision, both financially and emotionally.

So, trust your gut and embrace an agent who isn't afraid to ask the tough questions or offer insights you hadn't considered. It can make all the difference in your home-buying experience.

Key Questions to Ask When Interviewing a Real Estate Agent

When interviewing a potential real estate agent, asking the right questions will help you assess if they're the right fit for you. Even if you've already done your research, sending a quick email or having a phone conversation to ask a few targeted questions can be incredibly helpful. Below are some questions you might want to consider, based on what I'd personally ask when interviewing an agent:

1. How long have you been in the industry, and how is your team structured?

- This question gives you insight into their level of experience. Even if they're newer to real estate, a strong, experienced team can help bridge any knowledge gaps. An agent with a well-rounded team might offer more resources and support, ensuring a smoother transaction.

2. Are you a full-time or part-time agent?

- Full-time agents tend to have more availability and are often more immersed in the market's day-to-day changes. However, part-time agents can also be excellent, though their schedules may be more limited in terms of when they can show properties or attend meetings.

3. Do you work more with buyers, sellers, or both?

- Some agents specialize in working primarily with buyers or sellers, while others work with both. If you're buying, an agent who has more experience with buyers will better understand your needs and can offer a more tailored experience.

4. What's the best advice you give your clients?

- This question offers insight into their approach and whether they bring thoughtful, meaningful advice to the table. The depth of their response can show you how well they understand the complexities of the real estate process.

5. What do you love most about your job?

- You want to work with someone who enjoys what they do! Passionate agents are often more motivated and committed to helping you find the right home. This question helps reveal whether they genuinely enjoy real estate or if it's just a job to them.

6. Do you have any special expertise or niche focus?

- Just like my personal story about choosing an agent who specialized in land, this question is important if you have specific needs. For example, if you're looking for a property in a particular area, with acreage, or in a historic district, you want an agent who has expertise in those types of properties.

7. Do you work as an individual agent, or are you part of a team?

- Solo agents and team agents both have their advantages. Team agents may have additional resources and backup when they're unavailable, while individual agents might offer a more personal, hands-on experience. Ask about how the team structure impacts their ability to serve you.

8. What is your availability?

- This is crucial, especially if your schedule requires flexibility. If you can only view homes during nights and weekends, you need an agent who can accommodate that. Make sure to clarify their availability upfront to avoid scheduling conflicts.

9. How do you communicate with clients?

- Whether you prefer phone calls, emails, or texts, understanding how and how often an agent communicates is important. A good agent should match your communication style and keep you in the loop throughout the buying process.

10. What resources do you use to stay up-to-date on the market?

- Real estate is a fast-paced industry, and the market changes frequently. A good agent should be actively engaged in learning about new market trends, regulations, and local developments. Their ability to stay informed can greatly benefit you.

Bonus: What makes you different from other agents?

- This open-ended question gives them a chance to tell you what sets them apart, whether it's their knowledge, negotiation skills, or local expertise. Their answer will help you gauge if they're a standout agent or just one of many.

By asking these questions, you'll get a clearer sense of the agent's experience, work style, and how well they align with your needs. This process helps ensure that the agent you choose will provide the level of service and expertise you require throughout your home-buying journey.

Buyer Representation Agreement: What You Need to Know

As of **August 17, 2024**, new regulations from the **National Association of Realtors (NAR)** require buyer agents to have a **written agreement** with their clients before showing homes. This **Buyer Representation Agreement** is essential to clarify the terms, costs, and expectations of the relationship between the buyer and the agent. Here's a breakdown of why this agreement is important, what it entails, and what to watch for when signing one.

Why Do Agents Require a Buyer Representation Agreement?

In real estate, agents generally work on a **commission-only basis**, meaning they only get paid if you buy a home through them. If you're working with multiple agents without an agreement in place, each agent is dedicating time and resources without any guarantee that they will be the one to close the deal.

Signing a Buyer Representation Agreement shows your **commitment** to working with just one agent. This allows the agent to fully focus on helping you find the right property, knowing that their efforts are appreciated and will eventually be compensated.

- **Agent Commitment**: By signing, you're letting the agent know that you're serious, and in return, they can devote more time and resources to your search.
- **Protection for Agents**: This agreement prevents agents from doing a lot of work only to lose the sale to another agent, which can happen if buyers aren't loyal to a single representative.

What to Ask Before Signing

Before committing, make sure you're comfortable with the terms. One critical question to ask is:

Will You Release Me from the Agreement If I'm Unhappy?

It's important to discuss what happens if the relationship isn't working out. A reputable agent should have no problem agreeing to release you if you're unhappy with the service. This ensures you have **flexibility** if things don't go as planned and that you aren't locked into a contract with an agent who may not be meeting your needs.

How It Benefits You

For buyers, signing a Buyer Representation Agreement ensures that you:

- **Receive full attention** from your agent.
- Get **professional advice** on the best homes and deals.
- Establish a clear understanding of the terms and expectations.

It also opens the door for better communication, ensuring both you and the agent are aligned throughout the home-buying process.

In conclusion, a **Buyer Representation Agreement** fosters clear communication, mutual respect, and sets a strong foundation for a productive working relationship. Before signing, make sure to discuss the terms thoroughly and ensure you're comfortable with the arrangement. Know that due to these new requirements, an agent is unable to show you a home prior to an agreement being signed.

Chapter 8: Search for Your Perfect Home

You've done the groundwork—now comes the exciting part: **finding your perfect home.** Whether you're searching on your own or with a real estate agent, this is where you'll need to focus on your **must-haves, deal breakers**, and knowing what to overlook.

In this section, we'll discuss how to refine your criteria, provide examples of what to prioritize, and share some insights on navigating multiple offers.

Must-Haves: What You Can't Live Without

Before diving into house hunting, it's crucial to sit down and define your **must-haves**. These are the non-negotiables that will help you filter out properties that don't meet your needs. Must-haves typically include:

- **Location:** What's the right neighborhood or proximity to work, schools, or amenities?

- **Number of bedrooms and bathrooms:** How many do you need to comfortably accommodate your household?
- **Outdoor space:** Do you want a large yard, a pool, or no outdoor maintenance at all?
- **Home utilities:** Would you prefer gas, electric, or propane? Note: In some areas, you may not have a choice.
- **Special features:** Is a home office, open floor plan, or a big kitchen essential to you?

It's important to discuss these priorities with everyone involved in the purchase (spouse, partner, family). Aligning on these basics early will save you time and energy as you search.

Story Time: Avoiding House Hunting Fatigue

Let me tell you about Sam and Rachel, a couple who were excited to find their dream home but quickly found themselves overwhelmed. Without a clear plan, they started looking at dozens of properties, hoping something would just "feel right."

The problem was, they didn't have a firm idea of what they really needed. They weren't sure how many bedrooms they wanted, whether they wanted a pool, or even which neighborhood they preferred. Week after week, they toured house after house, trying to keep track of the pros and cons of each one. It wasn't long before the excitement turned into frustration.

By the time they came to us, Sam and Rachel were experiencing serious house-hunting fatigue. They felt like they'd seen every home on the market and were no closer to making a decision.

We knew it was time to refocus. Together, we sat down and created a list of their must-haves. How many bedrooms did they really need? Was a pool essential or just a nice-to-have? What location worked best for their daily routines? Once they committed to these priorities, everything changed.

With a clear vision in mind, Sam and Rachel were able to narrow down their search. They found a home that ticked all their must-have boxes and closed on it shortly after. The entire process became smoother and, most importantly, enjoyable again.

The Lesson

House-hunting fatigue is real, but it's avoidable. The key is to clarify your must-haves early in the process. While flexibility is important, having a clear sense of your priorities will help you stay focused and prevent the search from becoming overwhelming.

Most people already have a general idea of what they need—it's just a matter of committing to it. Work with your mortgage expert or realtor to create a focused list, and you'll find the home-buying process much more efficient and rewarding.

Deal Breakers: What to Avoid

Next, identify your **deal breakers**—things that would prevent you from seriously considering a property. Examples of deal breakers include:

- **Size:** Too big or too small? Know your limit on square footage.
- **School district:** This is a major factor for many buyers.
- **Major repairs:** Some people want move-in ready, while others are looking for fixer-uppers.
- **Natural disaster risk:** Is the property in a flood zone or an area prone to wildfires or hurricanes?

Just like must-haves, deal breakers may shift as you go through the process. It's okay to change your mind as you view homes and realize what truly matters to you.

Story Time: Changing Deal Breakers

When I started my own home-buying journey, I was convinced that I needed at least 2–3 acres of land, maybe even more. I had visions of wide-open space, privacy, and the tranquility of a large property. It was my number one must-have, and I didn't think anything else would feel right.

But as I began touring larger properties, reality set in. The sprawling land looked beautiful, but I hadn't fully considered the upkeep. Mowing the lawn alone would take hours, not to mention maintaining the landscaping or dealing with repairs on a property that size. It quickly became clear that the upkeep would be more overwhelming than peaceful.

That's when my deal breaker shifted.

I realized I didn't need several acres to achieve the peace and quiet I was looking for. I ended up buying a home with just under an acre of land. It was the perfect balance—enough space to feel serene and private but manageable enough to fit my lifestyle.

The Lesson

Sometimes, your deal breakers or must-haves will evolve as you go through the home-buying process. Touring properties and envisioning your daily life in each one can teach you a lot about what works—and what doesn't—for your lifestyle.

Be open to that change. Flexibility allows you to refine your priorities and find a home that truly fits your needs, even if it looks a little different than what you originally imagined.

Let's talk about things you should **overlook** when searching for your perfect home. If you've ever watched *House Hunters* (and let's be honest, most of us have), you've probably seen buyers get hung up on the most trivial details, like ugly paint colors. Here's the thing: **paint color** should be the last thing you worry about! Paint is one of the **easiest and cheapest changes** you can make to a home, and it shouldn't distract you from seeing the property's true potential.

Yes, painting can take time, and hiring a painter can add some cost, but it's an expense you can often **negotiate** into your purchase. What's important to remember is that paint is temporary, while key features like the **location, floor plan, and lot size** are permanent. You can't change where the house is, but you can always change the color of the walls.

A lot of first-time buyers get hyper-focused on surface-level aesthetics. Here's a tip: **look beyond the minor cosmetic issues**. Focus on the parts of the home that matter most and are expensive to change. Overlooking things like paint color or light fixtures can open up a world of opportunity for finding a home with solid bones and great value.

Minor Settling: What You Shouldn't Worry About

One thing you definitely don't need to stress over is minor settling. Every house, no matter where it's located, experiences some degree of settling over time. Settling occurs as the ground beneath your home naturally shifts, which is a normal and unavoidable process. Whether you live in earthquake-prone California or in

Texas, where the soil is particularly clay-rich and prone to shifting a little settling is bound to happen.

Now, this isn't to say you should ignore major foundation issues. However, if you notice minor settling—like small cracks in the walls or ceiling—it's often nothing to worry about. In fact, these little signs of movement are common in homes across the country. What's important is being able to differentiate between typical settling and more serious structural concerns. This is where having a trusted expert, such as a structural engineer or home inspector, comes in handy. They can help determine whether those small cracks are just cosmetic or indicative of a deeper issue.

To give you a real-life example, here in Texas, we deal with a lot of settling due to our clay-heavy soil, which my dad likes to call "gumbo soil." It's thick, retains moisture, and causes homes to shift slightly as the soil expands and contracts. When we owned a home, there was a lot of construction happening nearby, and we started to see some minor hairline cracks appear on the ceiling. At first glance, this might make anyone panic and think the house is about to fall apart. However, we took the responsible route and hired a structural engineer to take a look.

After an inspection, the report showed that everything was perfectly fine—the foundation was solid, and the cracks were simply the result of minor settling. The house was doing exactly what houses do: adjusting to its environment. Knowing this brought us peace of mind, and we didn't have to spend a fortune on unnecessary repairs.

The key takeaway here is to stay calm when you notice minor signs of settling. Most of the time, it's just a natural process, and it's something that a good home inspection can clarify. You don't want to get caught up in minor details that might not matter in the long run.

Don't Sweat the Small Fixes

Another thing to keep in mind is that some issues are incredibly easy to fix, even if they initially seem daunting. I understand that "easy" is a relative term, and not everyone is naturally handy. You might be thinking, *"But Jacqueline, I'm not good at changing out a faucet or installing a new light fixture!"* I totally get that. But here's the thing: if it's something you can buy at your local hardware store for a small amount of money, and either you or someone else can install it without breaking the bank, don't let it be a dealbreaker.

Yes, what's considered "easy" can vary from person to person, but that's where the expertise of your real estate agent comes into play. This is the perfect time to ask questions. Don't hesitate to raise your hand and say, *"Mr./Mrs. Realtor, is this something I should actually worry about? Is it an easy fix, and how much would it cost?"*

If you've chosen a good real estate expert, they will have the experience to give you a realistic answer. While some agents might not guarantee exact costs, a quick phone call to your trusted realtor, lending expert, or even a simple Google search will likely give you a good ballpark figure. That way, you can confidently decide if the fix is worth stressing over or if it's something minor that can be easily handled after the sale.

Don't Get Hung Up on Ugly Furniture

One of the easiest things to overlook during your home search is ugly furniture. And why should you? After all, guess what—you're not keeping it! Whatever furniture is currently in the house is going with the sellers when they leave. Unless you're buying a fully furnished home, which is more common with second homes or investment properties, you shouldn't let the seller's decor sway your decision.

It really doesn't matter if their couch is a burnt orange eyesore and you're a die-hard Texas A&M fan who would never let that color into your home. The ugly couch is leaving with them! Most of the time, sellers aren't including their furniture in the sale, so if you find it horrendous, remember it's not staying.

Story Time: Looking Beyond Cosmetic Issues

Let me tell you about Amanda, a client who was on the hunt for her dream home but kept getting stuck on minor details. She was working with a very savvy realtor, and together they toured house after house. However, Amanda couldn't seem to get past surface-level issues like ugly furniture, strange paint colors, and outdated ceiling fans.

No matter how hard the realtor tried to get her to focus on the home's potential, Amanda remained fixated on the aesthetics. Frustrated, the realtor finally asked me to jump on a call to help Amanda refocus.

When I asked her how the search was going, she said, "Well, it's fine, but we've seen a lot of ugly houses."

I chuckled and replied, "Okay, what's making them ugly in your opinion?"

Amanda responded, "Well, they have awful furniture and weird paint colors. One house had an electric blue ceiling fan in the kitchen—it was just bad."

I totally understood, but I asked her a critical question: "Would you rather buy a fully decked-out house with perfect furniture and pay $50,000 more, or would you prefer to spend $2,000 to $5,000 on paint and fixtures to customize it to your liking and save that money?"

Amanda hesitated, so I continued, "Here's the thing: a lot of other buyers aren't looking past that ugly paint and furniture either.

That's why this house is more affordable. You can walk away with instant value by customizing it and still coming out ahead."

Thankfully, Amanda listened. She took our advice, purchased one of the homes she had initially dismissed, and made it her own with a few affordable updates. A year later, when we helped her refinance, she had gained $80,000 in equity. The home was worth significantly more than what she paid for it, all because she looked beyond the surface-level flaws and saw the opportunity.

The Lesson

Amanda's story highlights why it's so important to focus on what truly matters when buying a home. Things like location, floor plan, and structural integrity are must-haves and dealbreakers. Cosmetic issues like paint, furniture, or light fixtures can be easily and affordably changed after you move in.

By looking past the surface-level flaws, you might find a home with hidden potential—and gain significant value in the process.

Next Step: Getting Set Up with an MLS Drip

Now that you've got your real estate agent on board, the next step is getting set up with what's called an **MLS drip**. This is a great tool that keeps you informed about new properties that match your specific criteria as soon as they hit the market.

What is an MLS Drip?

An **MLS (Multiple Listing Service) drip** is an automated system that your agent sets up for you. Once they input your parameters—like location, price range, number of bedrooms, etc.—the system will email you every time a property that fits those criteria is listed. This way, you'll always be up to date on the latest homes that meet your needs without having to manually search the market yourself.

Broad vs. Narrow Parameters

You can choose how broad or narrow your search parameters are. If your criteria are too broad, you'll likely be overwhelmed with listings, many of which won't be relevant. On the other hand, if you're too restrictive (e.g., looking in one small school district with very specific features), you may receive very few, if any, listings. The key is to strike a balance between what's essential and where you can be flexible.

Common Parameters Your Agent May Ask About:

- **Minimum and Maximum Square Footage**
    - If you want a certain amount of living space, like 1,500 sq. ft. or more, your agent will input that. Being flexible here can help if you're okay with a home slightly smaller or larger than your ideal.
- **Pool or No Pool**

- o If having a pool is a must (or something you want to avoid), let your agent know. This will filter listings accordingly.

- **Minimum Bedrooms and Bathrooms**
  - o The agent will ask how many bedrooms and bathrooms you need as a minimum. For example, if you need at least 3 bedrooms and 2 baths, they'll make sure you only receive homes that meet that.

- **Master Bedroom Location (Upstairs or Downstairs)**
  - o Some buyers prefer the master bedroom on the first floor, while others prefer it upstairs. If this is a priority for you, it's something your agent can add to the search criteria.

- **Specific Area, School District, or County**
  - o If location is your top priority, you'll need to specify the exact **school district**, **neighborhood**, or **county** where you want to search. Keep in mind that this could narrow your results significantly, especially in smaller areas.

- **Lot Size or Acreage**
  - o For buyers looking for more outdoor space, specifying a **minimum lot size** (e.g., 1 acre or more) will ensure the listings fit your needs.

- **Neighborhood or Community**

o   If there are specific neighborhoods you love, let your agent know so they can target those areas specifically.

Flexibility in Search Criteria

It's important to listen to your agent's advice when setting these parameters. They'll likely recommend avoiding too many restrictions at first because having overly specific criteria could limit the number of homes you see. A good approach is to focus on your **dealbreakers**—those must-have features that you won't compromise on—while being more flexible with the rest.

For example, if you're set on a specific school district, maybe you can compromise on square footage or the number of bathrooms. Your agent can always adjust the MLS drip as you refine your preferences.

It's Not Set in Stone

The great thing about an MLS drip is that it's not permanent. If after a few days or weeks, you feel the listings aren't quite right—whether too many or too few—your agent can **adjust the parameters**. It's a dynamic system designed to evolve with your search, ensuring you stay informed without feeling overwhelmed.

In summary, the MLS drip is a powerful tool to streamline your home search, but it's essential to balance your **must-haves** with flexibility to avoid missing out on great potential homes. Your agent will help you find the right balance and fine-tune the system as needed.

Navigating Multiple Offers: What You Need to Know

When the housing market gets competitive, it's common to encounter **multiple offer situations**. This means more than one buyer is interested in purchasing the same property, putting you in direct competition with other potential buyers. Multiple offer situations can be intense and fast-paced, so it's important to understand how they work and what strategies you can use to position yourself effectively.

What are Multiple Offers?

Multiple offers occur when several parties submit offers to purchase the same home. The seller is then in a position to choose which offer they find most attractive. This often leads to a bidding war, where buyers are encouraged to improve their offers in terms of price and terms to win the seller's favor.

Overbidding the List Price

One of the first things to understand in a multiple offer situation is that you may need to offer **above the list price** to stand out. Here's a simple example:

- Let's say a house is listed for $500,000. If the property generates significant interest and multiple offers are submitted, you might need to offer **$510,000, $520,000, or even $550,000** to increase your chances of winning the bid. However, be mindful of your budget and comfort level with overbidding.

Your **real estate agent** will help guide you through this process, providing insights into how competitive the market is and what type of offer is likely to succeed.

The Seller May Refuse to Cover Certain Costs

In a competitive market, sellers have more leverage, which means they might not agree to cover certain expenses that they normally would in a less competitive situation. For example:

- In Texas, it's typical for the seller to pay for title insurance. However, in a multiple offer scenario, the seller might ask the buyer to cover these costs instead. This is one way for the seller to maximize their profits and minimize their obligations.

Your agent can help you understand what costs you may be expected to cover and can negotiate on your behalf to strike the best possible deal.

"Highest and Best" Offers

When multiple offers come in, sellers often request a "**highest and best**" offer from each buyer. This means they are giving you a chance to improve your initial offer, but without knowing what other buyers have offered. The seller won't disclose the specifics of competing offers, but they are essentially saying, "If you want this house, make your best possible offer now."

You have to decide:

- **How much do you love this home?**
- **What's your maximum budget?**
- **Are you comfortable increasing your offer, or would you prefer to walk away?**

Financing Considerations in Multiple Offers

If you offer **above the list price**, it's important to understand the potential impact on your financing. If the home is listed at $500,000 and you offer $550,000, your lender will require the home to appraise for the amount you're borrowing. If the appraisal comes in lower than your offer, you might have to pay the difference out of pocket.

This is why it's crucial to work closely with your **mortgage expert**. They can explain what happens if the appraisal comes in low and whether you can finance the additional amount you've offered. Your mortgage expert will help you understand how much you can comfortably overbid and what financial limits you should keep in mind.

Everything is Negotiable

While it may feel like there's a lot of pressure in a multiple offer situation, it's important to remember that **everything is negotiable**. Even if the seller requests a highest and best offer, you don't have to change your initial offer if it's already at your maximum comfort level. The key is knowing your limits and working with your agent to craft an offer that's both competitive and within your budget.

Working with a Trusted Expert

One of the most important aspects of navigating multiple offers is having a trusted **real estate agent** and **lender** who can guide you through the process. They will help you evaluate the situation, provide strategic advice, and negotiate on your behalf to ensure you're making informed decisions. Real estate and mortgage transactions rarely go exactly as planned, so having experts who can adapt, solve problems, and offer sound advice is essential.

In conclusion, multiple offer situations require quick thinking, flexibility, and expert guidance. Knowing your limits, understanding the market, and working with experienced experts will help you navigate the complexities of competing for your dream home.

Beginning the Loan Process

Congratulations! You got your offer accepted and are now **under contract**—one of the most exciting milestones in your home-buying journey. While it's a thrilling moment, there are a few important next steps to focus on as you begin the **loan process** to finalize the purchase of your home. During this phase, you'll encounter several upfront fees that are essential to moving forward. Below is a high-level overview of what to expect, though keep in mind that some fees may vary depending on your state or the specific details of your transaction.

Upfront Fees: What to Expect

Here are some of the typical fees you'll encounter during this stage:

- **Earnest Money Deposit (EMD)**
- **Inspection Fees**
- **Appraisal Fee** (More details below)
- **Option Fee** (Applicable in Certain States, Like Texas)

Understanding Earnest Money and Inspections

As you begin the loan process, there are a few key upfront costs you'll need to handle. Two of the most significant are **earnest money** and the **inspection fee**. Let's take a closer look at what each entails and how they may vary depending on your location and situation.

Earnest Money Deposit (EMD)

Earnest money is a deposit you pay to show the seller you're serious about purchasing the property. It essentially takes the home off the market while the transaction proceeds. The amount of earnest money required can vary widely depending on several factors, including:

- **Your state**: The norms for earnest money differ across states. For instance, in **Texas**, it's common to pay around **1% of the purchase price** as earnest money. However, this amount could be higher—anywhere from **2-5%** or more—depending on market conditions, competition for the property, and the terms you negotiate.
- **Market conditions**: In a competitive, seller's market, offering **more** than the standard percentage can make your offer more attractive. On the flip side, in a buyer's market, you might get away with offering **less** than 1%.
- **Negotiation**: Your real estate agent will guide you on the best amount to offer. In some cases, offering a larger earnest money deposit shows that you're serious, which can help in a competitive offer situation.

If the transaction goes smoothly, the earnest money is applied toward your down payment or closing costs. If the deal falls through due to reasons allowed under the contract (like a failed inspection or financing issues), you may be able to get the earnest money back. However, if you back out for reasons not covered in the contract, you risk losing the deposit.

Home Inspection

Unlike earnest money, a **home inspection** isn't required by your lender but is highly recommended to protect your investment. The inspection is a comprehensive review of the home's condition and can help you identify any potential issues before you finalize the purchase. Here's what to keep in mind:

- **Not required by lenders**: Although your lender won't ask for an inspection, it's strongly advised so you know exactly what you're getting into. The inspection will look at the home's structure, electrical systems, plumbing, and other critical areas.
- **Inspection costs vary**: The cost of an inspection depends on what you want to be inspected. A **standard inspection** usually covers the basics (general foundation, roof, HVAC, etc.), but if you need **additional inspections** (like pools, irrigation systems, septic systems, or mold inspections), expect the cost to rise accordingly.
- **State-specific factors**: In Texas, for example, homes often have pools or larger land plots with septic systems, which

would require additional inspections. You'll pay more for these extra inspections, but it's worth it for peace of mind.

Your real estate agent can help you decide which inspections are necessary for your specific property. While it may seem like an added cost upfront, catching potential issues before they become larger problems will save you money and headaches in the long run.

The Appraisal: Costs

When you're using a mortgage to purchase a home, an **appraisal** is a critical step in the process. The appraisal is required by the lender to ensure the home's value aligns with the amount you're borrowing. While I'll go into more detail later about the appraisal process and its significance, here's a quick overview of what you need to know right now.

When Will You Pay for the Appraisal?

You'll typically need to pay for the appraisal **within the first week** of being under contract. It's important to budget for this upfront cost because it's required early in the process to move the loan forward.

Cost of an Appraisal

Appraisal fees can vary widely based on several factors, including:

- **Location**: The cost of appraisals depends on where you're buying. In some areas, you may pay as little as **$600**, while in others, the cost could be closer to **$1,500**. (In some cases you may need two appraisals, but it is rare.)
- **Type of property**: More complex properties—such as large estates, rural properties, or homes with unique features—may require a more detailed appraisal, which can increase the cost.
- **Type of appraisal**: Certain loan types (like **FHA** or **VA** loans) may require more in-depth appraisals, which can affect the price.

The Option Fee: A Texas-Specific Advantage

If you're buying a home in **Texas**, you'll likely encounter an **option period**, which is a unique aspect of the home-buying process in the state. The **option fee** is a small amount of money that allows you to put the property under contract and temporarily take it off the market while you conduct inspections or decide whether to move forward with the purchase. Not all states offer this, but it's a valuable tool in Texas real estate transactions.

What is the Option Fee?

The **option fee** is paid to the seller in exchange for the **option period**, which typically lasts between **5 to 10 days** (though the length can be negotiated). During this time, you can:

- Conduct a **home inspection** or any other evaluation.
- **Renegotiate** with the seller based on inspection findings.
- **Change your mind** and back out of the contract for **any reason**, without risking your earnest money (though the option fee is non-refundable).

This option period gives you a flexible window to decide whether you want to fully commit to the property, allowing for further due diligence without the pressure of immediately being locked into the purchase.

Cost of the Option Fee

The **option fee** varies based on factors like market conditions and the property itself. While there isn't a fixed rule, it typically ranges from **$200 to $500** or more. In competitive markets, offering a higher option fee can make your offer more appealing to sellers, showing them you're serious about the property.

Importance of the Option Period

The option period is incredibly useful because it provides you with the **flexibility** to walk away from the deal if you uncover issues during the inspection or if you simply change your mind. During this time, you won't risk your larger earnest money deposit, which is often a bigger financial commitment.

State-Specific Details

Keep in mind that not every state has an option period or option fee. If you're purchasing a home outside of Texas, it's important to check with your **real estate expert** about whether similar contingencies exist in your state. They can guide you on alternative protections, such as inspection contingencies, that offer some level of buyer security.

Consult Your Experts

For the most accurate information regarding fees—whether for the **option period**, **earnest money**, or **appraisals**—it's always best to reach out to your **mortgage** or **real estate expert**. They have detailed knowledge of the specific costs and requirements for your state and local market and can provide you with a clearer picture of the financial obligations based on your situation.

In summary, while the **option fee** and **option period** are unique to Texas, they are valuable tools that allow buyers to perform due diligence and make informed decisions. If you're in a state where option periods are available, it's an excellent safeguard to consider when entering a real estate contract.

Chapter 9: What Happens After You're Under Contract: A High-Level Overview of the Loan Process

Once you're under contract on your home, the **loan process** officially begins. Your **mortgage expert** and mortgage team will handle most of the heavy lifting from here, but it's helpful to know what's happening behind the scenes so you can stay prepared and organized. Here's a breakdown of what to expect:

1. Loan Product and Terms Selection

- **What Happens:** Once your mortgage expert receives your signed contract, they'll work with you to finalize your **loan product** and **terms**. This includes determining whether you're going with a **fixed-rate** or **adjustable-rate mortgage (ARM)**, the loan term (e.g., 15-year or 30-year), and any other product details.

- **What You'll Do:** Be prepared to discuss your goals and preferences so your mortgage expert can guide you toward the best product for your needs.

2. Rate Lock or Float Decision

- **What Happens:** You'll need to decide whether to **lock your interest rate** or **float** it. Locking means securing the current rate for a set period, while floating allows you to wait and see if rates improve before locking in. They also have the potential to get worse.
- **What You'll Do:** Your mortgage expert will help you weigh the pros and cons of locking versus floating, depending on market conditions and your timeline.

3. Initial Disclosures

- **What Happens:** Your mortgage expert will send you a set of **initial disclosures**. These documents outline the loan terms, fees, and estimated closing costs. You'll need to review and sign these to move forward.
- **What You'll Do:** Review these disclosures carefully. If anything seems unclear, ask your mortgage expert for clarification before signing.

4. Title and Appraisal Ordered

- **What Happens:** The **title company** will be asked to conduct a **title search** to ensure there are no legal issues with the property's ownership. Simultaneously, an **appraisal** will be ordered to determine the home's fair market value.

- **What You'll Do:** Not much is required from you at this stage, but be aware that these processes are happening in the background.

5. Loan Processing

- **What Happens:** Your file will be assigned to a **loan processor**, who will gather any additional documentation needed, such as updated income statements, bank records, or employment verification. The loan processor acts as a liaison between you and the underwriter.
- **What You'll Do:** You may be asked to submit updated documents, so stay organized and respond promptly to any requests from the processor.

6. Underwriting

- **What Happens:** The underwriter will review all of your financial documents, the appraisal, and the title report to ensure that you meet the lender's guidelines. After this review, you'll receive a **conditional approval**.
- **What You'll Do:** The underwriter may ask for additional information or clarification, which your mortgage expert or processor will communicate to you. Be sure to provide any requested documents as quickly as possible to avoid delays.

7. Conditional Approval and Document Updates

- **What Happens:** After reviewing your file, the underwriter will issue a **conditional approval**, which means your loan is likely to be approved pending a few more conditions (e.g., final documents, explanations, or verifications).
- **What You'll Do:** Work with your loan team to provide any last required documents.

8. Initial Closing Disclosure (CD)

- **What Happens:** You'll receive an **Initial Closing Disclosure** (CD), which outlines the final terms of your loan, including the loan amount, interest rate, monthly payments, closing costs, and cash to close. You must receive this document **at least three business days** before your closing date.
- **What You'll Do:** Review this document carefully, making sure all the terms match what was agreed upon. If you notice any discrepancies, let your mortgage expert know immediately.

9. Appraisal Return

- **What Happens:** The **appraisal report** will be completed and sent to your lender. The appraisal determines if the home's value supports the loan amount. If the appraisal comes in lower than the purchase price, your mortgage expert and real estate agent will guide you on the next steps, which could include negotiating the price or covering the difference.

- **What You'll Do:** Be prepared for possible adjustments if the appraisal differs from the purchase price.

10. Final Underwriting and Clear to Close

- **What Happens:** Once any remaining conditions are met, your loan goes through **final underwriting**. After a final review, you'll receive a **Clear to Close**, meaning all conditions have been satisfied, and the loan is ready to proceed to closing.
- **What You'll Do:** Celebrate—you're almost done!

11. Final Closing Disclosure and Final Balance

- **What Happens:** Before closing, you'll receive the **Final Closing Disclosure (CD)**, which will confirm the exact amount of money you need to bring to closing, if any. It will also outline any final changes or adjustments.
- **What You'll Do:** Review this document one last time to ensure everything is accurate.

12. Closing and Funding

- **What Happens:** Finally, it's time to sign the paperwork and officially close on your home! You'll go to the **closing** and sign all necessary documents to complete the purchase.

Once the lender funds the loan, the property officially transfers to you.

- **What You'll Do:** Bring your ID, review the documents carefully as you sign, and provide any final payments as required.

This may seem like a lot of steps, but your **mortgage expert** and **real estate team** will handle most of the work behind the scenes. You'll need to stay in communication and respond promptly to requests for documentation, but otherwise, much of the heavy lifting will be done by your experts. They are there to ensure the process goes as smoothly as possible while keeping you informed along the way.

Understanding Important Contract Dates

When you're under contract to buy a home, there are several key dates you need to keep track of. These dates are critical to ensuring the process moves smoothly, and missing them could have serious consequences. Here's a breakdown of the essential dates you'll encounter in your contract:

1. Option or Inspection Date

The **option period** (or **inspection period**) is the window of time you have to conduct a **home inspection** and negotiate repairs or back out of the deal if something major is discovered. This is your chance to thoroughly evaluate the property's condition.

- **Option Date (Texas and some other states):** If your state has an **option period** (like Texas), this date is when your **option period expires**, meaning the time frame in which you can terminate the contract for any reason and still retain your earnest money (though the option fee is non-refundable).
- **Inspection Date (Other states):** In states without an option period, the **inspection date** refers to the deadline for getting the home inspected. You'll need to get any inspections completed and negotiate any repairs before this date to ensure you don't lose your earnest money if you want to cancel.
- **Why It Matters:** If there are major issues found in the inspection, you have the right to renegotiate or terminate the contract within this window without penalty. **Missing this date** means you might not have the ability to walk away from the deal or renegotiate for repairs.

2. Financing Contingency Date

The **financing contingency** is a critical protection for you as the buyer. This clause allows you to cancel the contract if you're unable to secure financing for the home by a specified date.

- **What It Means:** The financing contingency gives you time to secure your mortgage without the risk of losing your earnest money if your loan is denied. If for some reason you cannot qualify for the loan (e.g., the appraisal comes in too low, your financial situation changes or the lender cannot approve the loan), you can terminate the contract, and your earnest money will be refunded.
- **Why It Matters:** Missing the financing contingency date could mean you are still **legally obligated** to buy the home even if you can't secure financing, which could result in you losing your earnest money or even facing legal consequences.

3. Closing Date

The **closing date** is the big day when everything is finalized. This is when you officially take ownership of the property, sign all the necessary documents, and pay any closing costs or down payment.

- **What It Means:** By this date, your loan should be fully approved, your final walkthrough of the home completed, and the seller should have fulfilled any contract obligations. Once all the documents are signed and the loan is funded, ownership of the home is transferred to you.
- **Why It Matters:** You and the seller are working toward this date. Missing the closing date could result in penalties or

delays in taking possession of the property, and it may also have financial consequences depending on the terms of the contract.

Chapter 10: Selecting Your Loan Product and Locking in Your Interest Rate

One of the most important decisions you'll make during the home-buying process is selecting your **loan product** and deciding whether to **lock in your interest rate**. This is where your **mortgage expert** becomes an invaluable resource, as they will guide you through the different options and help you make informed decisions based on your financial goals and market conditions.

1. Choosing the Right Loan Product

Your first step is to choose the type of loan that best fits your needs. Here are a few common loan products:

- **FHA Loan (Federal Housing Administration):** This is a government-backed loan, ideal for first-time homebuyers or those with lower credit scores. It typically requires a smaller down payment (as low as 3.5%).

- **VA Loan (Veterans Affairs):** Available to eligible veterans, active-duty military, and their families. VA loans usually require no down payment and offer competitive interest rates, but you must meet specific service requirements.

- **USDA Loan (United States Department of Agriculture):** Aimed at buyers in rural areas, USDA loans offer no down payment and are ideal if you're purchasing a home in a qualifying rural area.
- **Conventional Loan:** This is a standard loan that isn't backed by the government. Conventional loans typically require a higher credit score and a larger down payment (often 5-20%), but they offer more flexibility in terms of property types and fewer restrictions. If you are a first-time buyer, you may be able to put as little as 3% down.

Your **mortgage expert** will help you understand which loan program is the best fit based on factors like your credit score, down payment, and the property location. It's one of their biggest and most important jobs.

2. Selecting the Loan Term

Next, you'll decide on the **loan term**, which is the length of time you'll take to repay the loan. The most common options are:

- **30-Year Fixed:** Offers lower monthly payments because the loan is spread out over 30 years. However, you'll pay more interest over the life of the loan.

- **15-Year Fixed:**

  You'll pay off the loan in half the time, with higher monthly payments but less total interest. This is ideal if you can afford higher payments and want to build equity faster.

There are also adjustable-rate mortgages (ARMs), where the interest rate changes after a certain period, but these are less common for buyers looking for long-term stability. Your mortgage expert should have asked enough questions to determine if an ARM may be a good fit.

3. Locking vs. Floating Your Interest Rate

The final decision is whether to **lock in your interest rate** or **float** it. This can be a tricky decision, and it's where your mortgage expert's advice is crucial.

- **Locking Your Rate:**

  When you lock in your rate, you secure the current interest rate for a specified period (usually 30 to 60 days). This protects you from market fluctuations and ensures you know what your monthly payment will be. Locking is often recommended if rates are low or expected to rise.

- **Floating Your Rate:**

  Floating means you choose not to lock your rate right away, in hopes that interest rates will drop before closing. This can be risky because rates could rise, increasing your monthly payment. However, if the market indicates that rates might fall, floating could work in your favor.

Consult with Your Mortgage Expert

While this may seem like a lot of information, your **mortgage expert** will walk you through all these options, explaining the pros and cons of each. They'll help you determine the best loan product, loan term, and interest rate strategy based on your unique situation and market conditions.

Though the process may feel complex, your mortgage expert will help simplify these decisions and ensure you're making smart, informed choices.

Understanding Initial Disclosures: What They Are and Why They Matter

Once your loan product, interest rate, and loan term have been settled, the next step is receiving a packet called **initial disclosures**. This is a key part of the mortgage process, and while it may seem overwhelming at first, it's important to know what these documents entail and how to handle them.

What Are Initial Disclosures?

Initial disclosures are a set of documents sent to you by your lender, outlining the **specifics of your loan**. These documents are intended to give you a detailed overview of the loan terms and ensure that you understand the agreement you're entering into. The package often includes several standard legal documents, many of which are there as a result of past legal issues (hence the nickname "CYA" or **cover your ass** documents).

What's Inside the Initial Disclosure Package?

The package will include:

- **Loan Estimate (LE):** This document provides an itemized breakdown of your loan terms, including the interest rate, loan amount, estimated monthly payments, and closing costs.
- **Disclosures required by law:** These include forms explaining various aspects of the mortgage process, such as privacy policies, intent to proceed, and any other relevant consumer protection disclosures.
- **Other documents specific to your situation:** Depending on the loan type, state, or lender, there may be additional disclosures specific to your transaction.

While the package can be large, the goal is to protect both you and the lender by ensuring full transparency. Most buyers **e-sign** the disclosures, making the process easier and quicker.

What Should You Look For?

As you go through the documents, it's important to check for **initial errors** or anything that seems off, such as:

- Incorrect **loan terms** or **interest rate**
- Mistakes in your **personal information** (like your address)
- Errors in the **property details** or **loan product**

If you spot any errors, **raise your hand** and ask your mortgage expert for clarification. This is the time to correct any mistakes or misunderstandings before things move forward.

Important Tip: Sign Even If There Are Errors

Here's the part that often confuses clients: **even if you find errors**, most lenders will ask you to **sign the initial disclosures anyway**. This is because federal regulations require lenders to send out the initial package within a specific time frame after the loan terms are discussed and the contract is in place. Correcting errors in this package **doesn't delay the process**, but signing is necessary to keep the timeline moving.

Once you sign, your lender can work on correcting any issues you identified. They'll either send an updated disclosure package or confirm the adjustments.

Why Signing Is Critical: The Federal Timeline

The reason why signing is so important goes back to legislation passed after the **2008 mortgage crisis**—specifically, the **Dodd-Frank Act**. This law requires that borrowers are fully aware of their loan terms early on in the process, ensuring that there are no surprises at closing. Once you sign the initial disclosures, a **federal clock** starts, which ensures you have time to review the final terms before the loan is completed.

This process helps avoid situations where borrowers get to the closing table only to find out the loan terms aren't what they expected. It gives you a clear understanding of your mortgage terms **before** finalizing the deal. It's important to note that if you do want to make significant changes to the loan terms, there is still time to do this. Just get with your mortgage expert and they can make those adjustments. This will necessitate a new loan estimate to confirm those changes.

Story Time: Miscommunication and Federal Requirements

Let me tell you about David, a client who learned how important it is to stay engaged and sign initial disclosure documents promptly, even when you're still weighing your options.

David had been exploring several loan products with us, including FHA loans, conventional loans, and various interest rates. After much discussion, he finally went under contract on a home. This triggered a legal requirement for us to send out his initial disclosure package.

By federal law, lenders have a very tight deadline to send these documents, so we reached out to David multiple times to confirm his final choice of loan terms. Unfortunately, we didn't hear back in time. To meet the legal deadline, we had no choice but to send the disclosure package based on our initial discussions.

A few days later, David texted me: "Hey, I know we talked about getting an FHA loan initially, but I've decided that a conventional loan makes more sense for me now."

I replied, "That's totally fine, David, but I still need you to sign the initial disclosure package you received. Even though we're switching to a different loan type, federal law requires those initial documents to be signed as they were sent out."

David hesitated. "Why do I have to sign something that doesn't match what we're doing now?" he asked.

I explained, "I understand it might seem odd, but those initial disclosures are governed by strict federal rules. Signing them doesn't lock you into anything—it just ensures we're compliant and can keep the process moving. Once you sign, we can quickly send out an updated set of documents that reflect your final loan choice."

Thankfully, David signed the initial package, and within a couple of days, we sent him the revised disclosures for his conventional loan. The process moved forward without any delays, but it could have been derailed if he hadn't signed promptly.

Story Time: Catching Errors Early

Let me tell you about Karen, a client who learned how crucial it is to carefully review your initial disclosure package.

Karen had completed her loan application, and we had thoroughly verified all her information. Everything seemed to be in order—loan products, terms, and details had been discussed in depth. As required by law, we sent out her initial disclosure package.

When Karen received the documents, she noticed something unusual right away: the address listed for her current residence was completely wrong. The city had been imported incorrectly.

Karen called me immediately and said, "Hey, the address on the paperwork is incorrect. Is that going to cause a problem?"

"Good catch!" I told her. Because Karen flagged the issue early, we were able to correct it right away and reissue the documents without missing a beat. If she hadn't reviewed the disclosures carefully, this small error could have snowballed into a bigger issue later in the process, potentially causing delays or confusion.

The Lesson

Karen's story highlights why it's so important to review your initial disclosures thoroughly and flag any errors as soon as possible. While the paperwork might feel overwhelming with its legal jargon and fine print, catching mistakes early can save time, frustration, and potential setbacks down the line.

Most of the documents in the initial disclosure package are standard compliance forms—often called "CYA" or "cover your ass" documents. They exist to protect both you and the lender, ensuring that everything is accurate and transparent from the start.

So, take the time to review your disclosures carefully and sign them promptly. Staying engaged and proactive can make all the difference in keeping your loan process smooth and stress-free.

The one document you really want to focus on, though, is the **Loan Estimate (LE)**. This is your clearest window into the key details of your loan: the fees, the interest rate, whether that rate is locked or floating, and other important terms. While the Loan Estimate isn't a binding contract, it's an essential snapshot of what the lender is offering at that moment. Keep in mind that some elements can change over time, but it provides a solid foundation for understanding your loan's structure.

One thing to remember is that if you haven't communicated with your mortgage expert before the disclosures are sent out, the information might be outdated or incorrect. And yes, even if they contain errors, federal law still requires you to sign them within the set timeline. Those strict timing regulations I've mentioned before don't allow us to delay sending disclosures until every detail is ironed out. In short, time waits for no one in the mortgage process!

Signing your disclosures promptly keeps the process moving and ensures that any adjustments or corrections can be made later, without causing delays in your loan approval.

Mortgage Team Members: Key Players in Your Loan Process

During the mortgage process, you'll interact with several members of the loan team, each playing a crucial role in ensuring your loan application moves forward smoothly. Here's a breakdown of their roles and responsibilities.

1. Processor and Loan Assistant: Behind-the-Scenes Support

- **Role:** These individuals are responsible for reviewing your file and collecting all the necessary documents for your loan application. They play a key role in the middle stage of the mortgage process, ensuring that everything is in order for the underwriter's review.
- **Key Tasks:**
  - Collect documents such as pay stubs, bank statements, and other financial records.

- Order required reports, such as:
  - Title report
  - Property appraisal
  - Employment verification
  - Credit supplements
  - Property condition reports
- Ensure all documents are up-to-date before submission to the underwriter.

2. Document Updates and Requests

- **Updated Documents:** You may need to provide fresh copies of important documents if they are outdated or if any information has changed since your initial application. These could include:
  - Pay stubs
  - Bank statements
  - Proof of payments for earnest money or option money (if applicable based on your state).
- **Tip:** Keep track of document expiration dates and be prepared to submit updates promptly to avoid delays.

3. Homeowners Insurance Quote

- **Requirement:** At this stage, you'll need to secure a homeowners insurance quote, which will be a requirement for loan approval.
- **Options:**

- Many mortgage companies, including ours, offer courtesy quotes from trusted insurance providers.
  - Alternatively, you're free to choose your own insurance provider. Make sure to obtain the quote quickly, as processing times may vary between companies.

4. Team Guidance and Support

- **Assistance:** The processor, loan assistant, and other team members will guide you through each step, ensuring your paperwork is accurate, complete, and ready for underwriting.

By collaborating with these team members and promptly providing requested documentation, you'll help move your loan toward final approval.

Chapter 11: The Inspection Process

The inspection and underwriting steps often occur simultaneously during a real estate transaction. Let's break them down, starting with the inspection, as it's usually done first.

Property Inspection

While a property inspection is not typically required by the lender or mortgage company, it's highly recommended by most real estate professionals. Here's why:

A home inspection ensures that you're fully aware of any potential issues before making the largest financial transaction of your life. Since buying a home is such a significant investment, it's crucial to identify any hidden problems that could impact the value or safety of the property.

An inspector will examine the major systems of the house, including:

- **Structural components** (general foundation, roof, walls)
- **Electrical systems**
- **Plumbing**
- **HVAC (Heating, Ventilation, and Air Conditioning)**

If the property has special features such as a pool or a septic system, you may need a specialized inspector for those areas. Additionally, if you suspect any foundational issues, it's wise to bring in an expert in that field.

Why is it important?

The inspector's role is to identify any potential defects or safety issues, giving you the chance to address them before closing the deal. The last thing you want is to be blindsided by major repairs after the purchase.

While it's not mandatory, skipping an inspection could lead to expensive surprises down the road.

Choosing the Right Inspector

Here's how you can go about selecting a qualified inspector:

- **Ask your real estate agent:** They likely have trusted contacts who are familiar with the types of homes in your area.
- **Consult your mortgage company:** Some lenders may provide recommendations, though this is less common.
- **Search online:** Check reviews and ensure the inspector has good experience and knowledge of the area where you're purchasing the home. Regional expertise can be important, as housing structures and potential problems can vary by location.

What to Expect from an Inspection Report

An inspection report is meant to be thorough. However, it's important to remember that the inspector's job is to find issues — that's what you're paying them for. This means they will likely find problems, even with new construction homes. Don't be alarmed if the report is lengthy and detailed; many of the issues they flag may be minor and easily fixable.

Here are a few key points to keep in mind:

- **Common findings:** Expect to see items such as worn-out caulking, minor cracks, or cosmetic issues. These aren't necessarily deal-breakers.
- **Serious concerns:** Look out for issues related to the foundation, roof, or electrical systems, as these could require significant repairs.
- **Limitations of inspections:** Inspectors can't identify problems hidden behind walls or under floors unless there are visible signs. For example, if there's water damage behind a wall, they won't tear down the wall to investigate further.

The report helps you prioritize repairs or negotiate with the seller for necessary fixes before moving forward with the transaction.

Underwriting

Simultaneously, the underwriting process begins. This is where your lender assesses your financial situation to ensure that you qualify for the mortgage. While it happens behind the scenes, it's critical to keep the lines of communication open with your mortgage expert and quickly provide any documents they request to avoid delays in your approval.

In summary:

- **Inspection:** Focuses on identifying property issues and potential safety risks.
- **Underwriting:** Focuses on assessing your financial ability to meet mortgage obligations.

By carefully navigating both steps, you'll ensure you're making a sound investment without unexpected surprises.

Why Getting a Home Inspection is Important: The AC Story

Let me share a quick story that highlights just how essential a home inspection can be. We had a customer who went under contract to purchase a house. As part of the process, they decided to get a home inspection done. During the inspection, they discovered something unexpected—parts of the air conditioning system weren't properly connected, meaning the AC wasn't running correctly throughout the house. Now, this happened in Texas, a place where having a fully functioning AC is absolutely critical because of the intense heat.

Thanks to the inspection, the buyer was able to bring this issue to the seller's attention and negotiate for them to fix it—an expensive repair that might have gone unnoticed without the inspection.

The key takeaway?

You don't know what you don't know. Even the seller might not have been aware of this issue. A home inspection is designed to uncover potential problems before they become your responsibility, helping you avoid costly surprises.

The Importance of Inspections: The Old Wiring Story

Here's another story that highlights why an inspection is so crucial, especially when buying an older home. A close friend of ours purchased an older property and decided to have an inspection done. During the inspection, they discovered that the electrical wiring was extremely outdated and posed a significant fire risk due to its age. Because of this discovery, they were able to negotiate with the seller to get money for fixing the wiring after the purchase.

Why is this important?

Older homes often come with hidden safety hazards that aren't immediately visible, like outdated wiring or plumbing. An inspection brings these issues to light, allowing you to address them before they become dangerous or costly. As I mentioned earlier, you don't know what you don't know—and sometimes the seller doesn't know either.

An inspection could end up saving you time, money, and most importantly, help protect the safety of you and your family!

What Inspectors Can and Cannot Inspect

It's important to know that while inspectors are thorough, there are certain things they may not be able to inspect due to either lack of expertise or access. For example, some inspectors may be licensed to inspect specific features like pools or pool equipment, while others may not have the qualifications. The same goes for specialized systems like septic tanks—some inspectors are licensed to inspect them, while others will recommend that you bring in a specialist.

The good news is that inspectors will clearly notate any areas they were unable to inspect in the report. If they don't have the expertise to inspect a particular feature or system, they'll let you know so you can arrange for a qualified expert to evaluate that specific area.

Key takeaway:
Always review the inspection report carefully for any areas the inspector was unable to examine. This way, you can bring in

specialists as needed to ensure no aspect of the property goes unchecked.

Chapter 12: Understanding Underwriting, Conditional Approval, and Appraisal (all happening at the same time)

Let's dive into the underwriting process, conditional approval, and appraisal, starting with the role of the underwriter.

What is Underwriting and Why Does it Matter?

Underwriting is a critical step in the loan approval process. An underwriter is the person responsible for reviewing all the documents in your loan file to determine whether you're a good risk for the lender. Essentially, they are assessing your ability to repay the loan based on the information you've provided. Let me emphasize again: **everything in the loan process is risk-based.** The underwriter's main job is to assess the risk factors associated with approving your loan.

Think of the underwriter as a fact-checker. They verify that all the details in your loan file are accurate and in line with what's required by the automated underwriting system. They ensure that the income, assets, credit history, and other documents you've submitted match up with the lender's guidelines.

An Example and an Analogy

Let me simplify this with an example: Imagine you've stated on your application that you earn $75,000 per year, and you've submitted a couple of pay stubs to verify that. The underwriter's job is to check those pay stubs, possibly request more documentation (like tax returns or employment verification), and confirm that everything aligns with what was entered into the automated system. They are making sure that your information is accurate and meets the lender's criteria. In short, underwriting is about making sure everything checks out before the loan is fully approved.

Analogy: Imagine a friend comes to you asking to borrow some money. Naturally, before you agree, you want to make sure they're capable of paying you back. So, you ask your friend for some basic information: "How much money do you make? How have you been managing your bills? Can you show me proof that you'll be able to repay me?"

This is exactly what an underwriter does for a lender. The underwriter's job is to make sure that the lender feels confident you'll be able to repay the loan. They verify your income, check your credit history, and ensure that the loan terms make sense based on your financial situation. Just like you wouldn't want to lend money to someone who couldn't pay it back, the lender wants to be sure you can meet your loan obligations.

But Didn't We Already Do This at the Beginning?

You might be thinking, "Didn't we already go through this when I applied for the loan?" The answer is yes, but at the beginning, the process was automated. When you first applied, the lender used an **automated underwriting system** to quickly assess whether you generally qualify for the loan. This is like running a basic check, but it's not the final word.

At this stage, a **mortgage expert** reviews your application to ensure it passes the initial guidelines. However, when your file reaches the **underwriter**, a *real person* goes through all of your documents with a fine-tooth comb to confirm everything is in order and that you're a low risk for the lender.

So while the initial run-through gave you a good indication that you qualify, the underwriter's review is the final and more detailed check before the loan gets approved. Just like you would double-check everything before lending money to a friend, the underwriter makes sure everything is solid before the lender makes the loan.

Conditional Approval

Once the underwriter has reviewed your documents, they may issue a **conditional approval.** This means that the lender is willing to approve the loan as long as certain conditions are met. These conditions could include additional documentation, explanations, or even an appraisal.

Why is conditional approval important?

It's a sign that you're on the right track, but there are still a few more steps to take before final approval. Meeting these conditions is crucial to move forward with the process.

What Additional Documents Might Be Requested?

You might be wondering, "What additional things could they possibly ask for?" Here are some common requests underwriters make after issuing conditional approval:

- **Missing Documents:** If you hadn't gotten around to submitting certain documents, such as updated bank statements, pay stubs, or tax returns, they may request those now.
- **Clarification of Existing Documents:** If any of the documents you submitted raise questions or don't perfectly align with the lender's guidelines, they may ask for clarification or additional supporting information.

- **Pending Reports:** Sometimes, they are simply waiting on reports that are still in process, like the **appraisal** report or a **title report**, to confirm the property's value or verify ownership status.

The good news is that the underwriter should provide you with a clear list of exactly what they need to finalize the loan. This conditional approval is a sign that you're nearing the finish line—just a few more steps before the loan is fully approved!

Why It's Crucial to Be Honest and Thorough from the Start

This is why I emphasize the importance of working with someone who understands all the guidelines when applying for a loan. If any information was entered incorrectly or if you didn't fully disclose something upfront, this is the stage when it will come to light. The underwriter's job is to review your file in detail to ensure everything checks out—so it's critical that the information you provide is accurate and complete.

The Importance of Transparency

Remember when I said it's always better to tell us everything upfront? That's because once the underwriting process starts, the lender will be running multiple reports to verify your details:

- **Credit and financial reports:** To confirm your creditworthiness and financial history.
- **Property reports:** To check if you own other properties, and whether any issues are associated with them.
- **Fraud reports:** To identify any potential red flags, such as past fraudulent activity.

These reports will uncover any discrepancies or issues that weren't disclosed at the start. If something unexpected shows up, it can delay the loan or even result in denial. That's why it's so important to be open and provide all the necessary details right from the beginning.

Final Thought: Avoid Surprises in Underwriting

To avoid any unpleasant surprises during underwriting, make sure that all your financial information is accurate, and disclose anything that might affect your application. It will save you time, prevent delays, and ensure a smoother process overall.

Appraisal: A Critical Step in the Homebuying Process

The **appraisal** is a crucial and often misunderstood part of purchasing a home. Many buyers may not fully grasp its importance or necessity. Let's break it down.

What is an Appraisal?

An **appraisal** is an independent assessment conducted by a licensed professional to determine the fair market value of a property. This ensures that the home is worth the amount both the buyer and the lender are committing to. It's a safeguard for both the buyer and the lender to avoid overpaying for the property. (You, typically, will pay for the appraisal prior to it being ordered.)

Why Is an Appraisal Necessary?

The lender requires an appraisal to verify the home's value before approving a mortgage. It confirms that the property can serve as collateral for the loan. This step ensures that the buyer isn't paying more than the home is worth and that the lender is not taking on excessive risk by financing a home with an inflated value.

How Does an Appraisal Affect Your Loan?

- **If the appraised value matches or exceeds the purchase price**: The loan process proceeds as planned.
- **If the appraised value is lower than the purchase price**: The lender will only finance up to the appraised value, which could lead to the following:

- Renegotiation: You may renegotiate the price with the seller to match the appraised value.
  - **Pay the difference**: You may choose to cover the gap between the appraised value and the purchase price with additional funds.
  - **Walking away**: Depending on your contract, you could cancel the deal if the terms aren't favorable.

Is an Appraisal Always Required?

If you're financing your home with a mortgage loan, an appraisal is generally required. This step verifies the property's value to the lender.

Types of Appraisals

- **Traditional Appraisal**: A licensed appraiser physically visits the property to assess its condition and compares it with similar homes recently sold in the area. This is the most common form of appraisal.

- **Automated Appraisal**: In some cases, lenders use automated systems that generate an appraisal based on market data. This is less common and may only apply to specific types of loans.

What Happens if the Appraisal Value Differs from the Purchase Price?

- **Appraisal Comes in High**: If the appraisal exceeds the purchase price, you've instantly gained equity in the property.
- **Appraisal Matches the Purchase Price**: The transaction can move forward smoothly, as the property is deemed worth the purchase price.
- **Appraisal Comes in Low**: This scenario can complicate things, but there are options:
    - **Renegotiate the price** with the seller to match the appraised value.
    - **Cover the difference** out of pocket to bridge the gap between the purchase price and the appraisal.
    - **Meet halfway**: Negotiate a compromise where both the buyer and the seller share the difference.
    - **Walk away** from the deal if your contract allows it, based on the appraisal contingency.

Additional Option: Covering the Appraisal Gap

In competitive markets, buyers may choose to cover the difference between the appraised value and the purchase price. This happens when buyers value aspects of the home—like location or unique features—that may not be fully captured by the appraisal.

The Final Option: Canceling the Contract

If you're uncomfortable with renegotiating or paying the difference, you can cancel the contract. Though you won't be refunded any inspection or appraisal costs, this option helps protect you from overpaying for a property that doesn't meet the appraised value.

Real-Life Appraisal Scenarios: The $5,000 Shortfall

Let me tell you about Jack, a buyer who found himself in a tricky situation when the appraisal for his dream home came in lower than expected.

Most of the time, appraisals come in at or above the market value. But occasionally, they can fall short for various reasons—perhaps the property is unique and hard to value, or the seller was overly optimistic about its worth. Unfortunately for Jack, this was one of those times.

The appraisal for the property came in $5,000 lower than the agreed-upon purchase price. Jack, understandably, wasn't comfortable paying an additional $5,000 out of pocket to cover the difference.

This led to a conversation between the buyers' agent and the sellers' agent to see if there was room to negotiate. After some back-and-forth, the seller agreed to lower the price by $5,000, bringing it in line with the appraised value.

The outcome was a win-win:

- Jack was thrilled because he didn't have to pay extra out of pocket.
- The seller, while taking a small hit, was still able to sell the property without losing the deal.
- Both agents were happy because the transaction moved forward smoothly, without unnecessary complications.

The Lesson

While not every low appraisal scenario resolves this easily, Jack's experience highlights the importance of staying calm and working with your real estate team to find a solution.

When an appraisal comes in low, negotiation is often possible. A good agent can help facilitate conversations between the buyer and seller to reach a fair agreement that works for everyone.

This story is a reminder to trust your team and focus on the bigger picture—getting to the closing table with terms that leave you in a strong position to purchase your new home at a fair value.

The Role of Appraisal Waivers in a Competitive Market

In recent years, fluctuating market conditions have often required buyers to make offers significantly above the original listing price.

To remain competitive, buyers are sometimes encouraged to sign an appraisal waiver, a tool that can help secure a home in a hot market but comes with financial implications.

What Is an Appraisal Waiver?

An appraisal waiver is a form in which the buyer agrees to pay the agreed-upon purchase price, even if the appraisal comes in lower. This means that the buyer is willing to cover the difference between the appraised value and the purchase price out of pocket. There are two main types of waivers:

- **Partial Appraisal Waiver**: The buyer agrees to pay a set amount over the appraised value, but this amount is capped. For instance, if you agreed to cover up to $20,000 more than the appraised value, and the appraisal comes in $10,000 lower than the purchase price, you'd be required to pay that extra $10,000.
- **Full Appraisal Waiver**: The buyer agrees to cover the entire gap between the purchase price and the appraised value, with no cap on how much they might pay if the appraisal comes in lower.

Story Time: Appraisal Waiver

Let me tell you about Lauren and Chris, a couple navigating the red-hot real estate market of 2020. With homes flying off the market and bidding wars breaking out, they had already lost out on several offers and were determined to secure their dream home.

When they found the perfect property, they decided to go all in, offering $100,000 over the listing price and including a full appraisal waiver. This meant they were committing to pay the full purchase price, regardless of what the appraisal determined the home was worth.

When the appraisal came back, it valued the property at $20,000 less than their purchase price. For many buyers, this could have been a dealbreaker, as they would need to cover the $20,000 difference out of pocket.

Fortunately, Lauren and Chris were financially prepared for this possibility. They had sufficient funds to bridge the gap and brought the additional $20,000 to the table at closing. For them, the risk paid off—they finally secured their dream home after months of missing out in a fiercely competitive market.

The Lesson

Appraisal waivers can be a powerful tool in a competitive market, but they come with significant risks. If the appraised value comes in lower than the purchase price, buyers must be prepared to cover the difference out of pocket.

Conclusion: Stay Calm and Be Flexible

Appraisals can be nerve-wracking, but understanding the process and knowing your options can help you navigate any surprises. Whether it's renegotiating, covering the gap, or walking away, there are always solutions available to ensure you make the right decision for your situation.

Initial Closing Disclosure After Conditional Approval

Once the conditional approval is issued, most companies—though not all—will allow the **Initial Closing Disclosure (CD)** to be sent to the customer. This is an important document in the closing process, but it's crucial to understand what it represents and what it doesn't.

What is the Initial Closing Disclosure?

The Initial Closing Disclosure provides a similar breakdown of the costs associated with your loan compared to the **Loan Estimate** you received earlier in the process. While the Loan Estimate gives you a preliminary idea of fees and costs (essentially the lender's best guesses), the Initial Closing Disclosure should be much more definitive because, by this point, many of the actual costs and fees are clearer.

However, it's important to note that **the Initial Closing Disclosure is not necessarily 100% final or correct**. There could still be adjustments made between when you receive the initial CD and the final version you'll sign at closing.

How is the Initial Closing Disclosure Different from the Loan Estimate?

- **Loan Estimate:** This was part of the initial disclosure package, providing the lender's best estimates of the loan costs, fees, taxes, and insurance.
- **Initial Closing Disclosure:** This document is more refined and should give you a better picture of the actual closing costs. Many of the fees are finalized, but some may still change before closing. At this point the interest rate will be locked, it is a requirement prior to the initial closing disclosure going out.

The Initial Closing Disclosure is a key step in the process because it gives you more transparency into the loan's final terms and costs, allowing you to ask questions or clarify anything that doesn't look right before closing.

Why Might the Initial CD Not Be Fully Accurate?

- **Pending Conditions:** If there are still pending items related to your conditional approval (such as final reports or updated documents), some of the fees or costs might still be in flux.
- **Adjustments in Fees:** Fees for services like title insurance or closing costs may change slightly as final numbers come in from the title company or other parties.

In short, the Initial Closing Disclosure should be more accurate than your Loan Estimate, but it's not necessarily the final word. There's still room for adjustments, but it provides a clearer picture of what your final closing costs are likely to be.

Understanding What's Set in Stone with the Initial Closing Disclosure

At the point when you receive the **Initial Closing Disclosure**, several costs should already be finalized, or very close to it. For instance:

- **Appraisal Costs:** By now, the appraisal should be completed, and the cost will be clearly outlined on the disclosure.
- **Title Fees:** Most of the title fees should be known and included, although there may still be some minor adjustments before closing.
- **Interest rate:** It must be locked prior to this form reaching you.
- **Origination and Discount Charges:** These fees, which are paid to the lender for processing the loan or to reduce your interest rate, should be locked in and unlikely to change.

What to Do if You Spot Errors

If you review the Initial Closing Disclosure and something seems inaccurate or wrong, **this is the time to raise your hand**. Immediately notify your mortgage expert so they can investigate and either:

1. **Correct an error:** Sometimes, a mistake may have been made when entering or calculating fees, and it can be quickly fixed.
2. **Address a larger issue:** If the discrepancy is more significant, such as an unexpected increase in fees or an unresolved issue, your mortgage team will be able to address it before you move further in the closing process.

The Initial Closing Disclosure is meant to give you transparency into what your final costs will look like, but it's important to carefully review it and flag any concerns before you proceed to the next step.

The Initial Closing Disclosure: A Critical Document from Dodd-Frank

Both the Loan Estimate and the Initial Closing Disclosure forms are products of the Dodd-Frank Act, which was designed to increase transparency and protect consumers during financial transactions. This disclosure is incredibly important, and here's why you want to sign it as quickly as possible:

Why Timing Matters

Federal law mandates that you **cannot close on your home until a minimum of three business days after the Initial Closing Disclosure has been sent and signed**. It's essential to understand that these three days are *business days*, which means:

- **Sundays** and **federal holidays** don't count.
- **Saturdays** generally do count, giving you a bit more flexibility.

If you delay signing this form, it could push your closing date back, so it's in your best interest to review it quickly.

What If the Form Is Inaccurate?

If there's something wrong or inaccurate on the Initial Closing Disclosure, it's perfectly okay to raise the issue with your mortgage expert. They may be able to:

- **Correct the issue**: If it's an error, they might fix it immediately.
- **Cancel the current form and send a new one**: In some cases, the system may allow them to cancel the first form and issue a corrected version. However, there are times when their system won't allow them to cancel or pull back the document. In this situation, it's still important to sign the form to avoid delaying the closing. You can always address the inaccuracies before the final closing, and adjustments can still be made.

Signing the Initial Closing Disclosure: What It Means

It's crucial to note that **signing the Initial Closing Disclosure doesn't bind you to the loan or the purchase of the home**. Just like with the initial Loan Estimate, signing this document is part of the process, but it doesn't lock you into anything. You can still back out of the deal, even after signing the disclosure.

Can You Walk Away?

Yes, you have the right to walk away from the loan or the home purchase **up until the day of closing**. While this might incur some expenses (such as appraisal fees or earnest money deposits), you're not legally obligated to go through with the loan until you've signed the final closing documents. So, don't worry about signing an imperfect form—it's simply a step in the process, and adjustments can still be made before the final loan documents are signed.

In summary, signing the Initial Closing Disclosure quickly is important to keep your closing on track, but don't stress if there are minor inaccuracies. Communicate with your mortgage expert, and know that you're not fully committed to the purchase until the final paperwork is signed on closing day.

Story Time: Walking Away from a Dream Home at the Final Hour

Let me tell you about Emily, a first-time homebuyer who had done everything right. From the moment she started the mortgage process, Emily was meticulous—submitting every document on time, meeting all the deadlines, and working hard to ensure everything was in order. After months of dedication, she was just one day away from closing on her dream home.

Everything was set. The inspection was complete, the appraisal was finalized, and the paperwork was ready to go. Emily's excitement was palpable as she prepared to step into the next chapter of her life.

But then, the unthinkable happened.

The day before closing, Emily lost her job.

Her voice trembled as she called to explain what had happened. It wasn't just disappointment—it was devastation. For Emily, this home wasn't just a purchase; it was the culmination of her hard work and the start of a new chapter. But now, everything had changed.

We deeply sympathized with Emily's situation. Losing a job is hard enough, but losing it at such a critical moment felt particularly cruel. Together, we discussed her options, and it became clear that walking away was the most logical and responsible decision.

Without a steady source of income, Emily couldn't afford to take on the responsibility of a mortgage, no matter how much she loved the house. She had already signed the initial closing disclosure and had invested so much time, energy, and money into the process. However, she understood that going through with the purchase could jeopardize her financial future.

With immense strength and maturity, Emily made the difficult decision to walk away from her dream home the day before closing.

The Lesson

Emily's story is a heartbreaking reminder that unexpected life changes can derail even the most carefully planned home purchases. While the situation was devastating, Emily's decision to prioritize her financial stability was the right one.

Buying a home is an exciting milestone, but it's also a significant financial responsibility. Life happens, and when it does, it's important to approach these moments with clarity and focus on what's best for your long-term future.

If you're ever in a similar situation, remember: your mortgage expert is here to help guide you through the tough decisions. Walking away from a home might feel like the end of a dream, but it can also be the first step toward a stronger and more secure path forward.

The good news is that less than six months later, Emily secured a new job, found another home that was perfect for her, and closed on the perfect place!

The Final Approval Process

Once all the necessary reports, including the appraisal, have been completed and all required documents submitted, your mortgage expert will send your file back for final approval. At this point, the underwriter will review everything again to ensure that all outstanding conditions have been met and the file is complete.

What is Final Approval?

Final approval means the underwriter has reviewed the file one last time, confirmed that everything is in order, and signed off on the loan. They will check off any remaining tasks or conditions that need to be completed, such as updated documents or final verifications.

How Long Does Final Approval Take?

A common question people have is how long the final approval process takes, but the answer can vary based on several factors:

- The number of documents resubmitted: If there were many items that needed clarification or additional documentation, this could extend the timeline.
- How busy the lender is: If the lender has a large number of files in their system at that time, this can delay the process.
- When your closing is scheduled: Lenders generally prioritize files that are closer to their scheduled closing date.

Most of the time, you should receive final approval at least one to three days prior to closing. However, it's hard to give a definite answer because it depends on all these factors. There are rare occasions that all conditions have not been met and the loan will need to go back into underwriting. In which case, the new conditions would need to be satisfied, and the loan be re-submitted for the final loan approval again.

What You Can Do

If you're wondering how long your final approval will take, the best thing to do is ask your mortgage expert. They can give you an idea of when to expect final approval based on your file's specific circumstances and the current workload of the lender. While it's impossible to guarantee an exact timeframe, they should be able to provide a rough estimate.

In summary, while final approval generally takes place close to the closing date, how quickly it happens depends on factors like the complexity of the file and the lender's workload at the time.

Final Walkthrough: The Last Step Before Closing

Great news! You're now in the **homestretch**—final approval has been received, and you're just about ready to close on your new home. There's one last important step before the actual closing: the **final walkthrough**.

What is a Final Walkthrough?

The final walkthrough is your chance to do a final check of the property before closing. It's an opportunity to ensure that everything is in the condition you expect and that there haven't been any major changes or damage to the home since you went under contract. This step is essential for a few key reasons:

- **Verify Repairs:** If you requested repairs as part of your contract, this is your chance to ensure that they've been completed to your satisfaction.

- **Check for New Damage:** You'll want to make sure that no new damage has occurred to the property since the last time you saw it, such as water leaks, damage from moving out, or other issues that may have cropped up.

- **Confirm the Home's Condition:** This isn't the time to bring up small issues that you missed during the initial inspection. If there was something present at the time of the original inspection that you overlooked, it's generally considered too late to address it now. The walkthrough is to ensure nothing has changed or worsened since then.

Important Reminders for the Final Walkthrough

- **Attend if Possible:** While it's not mandatory for you to be there in person, it's highly recommended that you attend the walkthrough. You want to personally confirm that the home is in good condition. If you're an out-of-town buyer and can't make it, your real estate agent can do it on your behalf.

- **Timing:** The final walkthrough typically happens **24 to 48 hours before closing**. In some cases, it even takes place on the **same day** as closing. Timing is flexible, but it's crucial to have it done as close to closing as possible.

- **Who Will Be There:** Usually, your real estate agent will accompany you for the walkthrough. If your agent can't make it, they may send another agent from their team or arrange for the seller's agent to guide you through. Regardless, someone will assist you in reviewing the property.

What Happens If You Find an Issue?

If you discover a problem during the final walkthrough—such as unfinished repairs or new damage—you'll want to bring it up immediately with your agent. Depending on the severity of the issue, you can work with the seller to resolve it before proceeding with the closing. This may involve negotiating for additional repairs, compensation, or, in some cases, delaying the closing until the problem is addressed.

In summary, the final walkthrough is a crucial last step to ensure everything is as it should be. It gives you peace of mind before you finalize the purchase and sign the closing documents. Make sure to take your time, inspect the home thoroughly, and communicate any concerns right away.

Chapter 13: The Closing Process

Congratulations! You're almost at the finish line of your home-buying or refinancing journey. Now, it's time for the closing, where all the final paperwork is signed, and ownership of the property is officially transferred. Let's walk you through what to expect, keeping in mind that the process can vary slightly depending on the state.

What is Closing?

Closing is the final step in your real estate transaction. It's the official meeting where you'll sign the necessary documents to finalize your mortgage and transfer the property title. Afterward, the lender will fund the loan, and you'll become the official owner of the property.

Where Does Closing Happen?

The location of the closing can vary based on state regulations and your specific transaction. Here are the typical options:

- **Title Company**: In most states, closings are held at the office of a title company. The title company handles the paperwork and ensures the proper transfer of ownership.

- **Attorney's Office**: In some states, such as New York, closings must take place with an attorney present. These are known as "attorney states," where a lawyer facilitates the closing.
- **Lender's Office**: Occasionally, the closing may happen at your mortgage lender's office, though this is less common.
- **Mobile Notary:** Occasionally, a mobile notary or mobile attorney may be a possible option, although much less common.

Steps to Take Before Closing

1. **Raise Concerns Early**: If you anticipate that you can't attend the closing in person or any other possible delays, let your real estate agent and lender know immediately to arrange for possible accommodations.
2. **Review Documents**: Before the closing date, review all the documents provided. This includes any loan documents already provided, the final closing disclosure, and anything title or your real estate team may have provided you.
3. **Ask Questions**: If you're unsure about any part of the closing process, reach out to your real estate agent, attorney, or mortgage expert. They're there to guide you through every step.

Remote Closings

If you can't attend the closing in person, a **remote closing** may be an option. Some states allow you to sign documents remotely, but this can sometimes delay the process, so it's critical to inform your mortgage expert and realtor ahead of time. Arrangements for remote closings may take extra time, so give as much notice as possible if you need to do this.

Hybrid and Electronic Closings

Some states allow part of the closing process to be done electronically, but certain key documents (usually 4-5) still require a hand-signed signature. Even if electronic signatures are allowed for some forms, your state or the title company might insist on traditional signatures for certain important documents. You may experience a **hybrid closing**, where part of the paperwork is signed electronically, and the rest in person.

How Much Money Do You Need to Bring to Closing?

The exact amount you need to bring will be detailed in your final **Closing Disclosure**, which you should receive at least 24 hours before closing. This document outlines all the costs, including interest rates, fees, and the total amount required for the transaction.

Although an **initial closing disclosure** is sent out earlier in the process, the final version will give you a precise number. It's crucial to follow the instructions from your title company, attorney, or lender to ensure you bring the correct amount and understand the payment method.

How to Bring Funds to Closing

You won't be bringing cash or personal checks to the closing table. Instead, you'll need to bring a **cashier's check** or arrange a **wire transfer**. Be sure to confirm with whoever is handling the closing (whether it's the title company or attorney) how they prefer to receive the funds. This step is critical, as mistakes in transferring money can cause delays.

Story Time: The Importance of Knowing How to Bring the Money

Meet Greg, a homebuyer who was thrilled to be closing on his new home just days before Christmas. With the holiday spirit in full swing, Greg was excited to spend his first Christmas in his new home, planning to move in over the weekend and celebrate with family and friends.

The closing was scheduled for Friday, and everything seemed to be on track. However, despite repeated reminders to confirm the acceptable form of payment with the title company, Greg didn't follow through.

On the day of the closing, Greg arrived with a cashier's check, believing it would be sufficient. Unfortunately, the title company handling the transaction had a strict policy requiring 48 hours to verify cashier's checks before finalizing any closings.

This meant the funds couldn't be verified before the weekend, delaying the entire transaction. Greg couldn't get the keys to his new home and had to postpone his move-in plans.

Greg was understandably frustrated, but the title company's policy was firm—they couldn't finalize the deal without verifying the funds. The delay left Greg stuck in limbo, unable to move in until after the holiday.

This unfortunate situation could have been avoided with one simple step: confirming with the title company beforehand what forms of payment they accepted. A wire transfer or other verified method would have ensured the funds were cleared on time, allowing Greg to close as planned and enjoy Christmas in his new home.

The Lesson

Greg's experience highlights the importance of communicating with your title company or attorney's office well in advance of closing. Policies regarding acceptable payment methods can vary, and misunderstanding them can result in frustrating delays at the final hour.

If you're unsure about anything—how to deliver funds, what documents are needed, or how the process works—don't hesitate to ask. Taking a moment to clarify expectations with the experts helping you is far better than risking a delay when you're so close to the finish line.

Remember: small steps can make a big difference in ensuring a smooth and successful closing day.

Conclusion: A Story That Ties It All Together

To bring everything full circle, let me share the story of Lonnie, a client whose home-buying journey was a perfect example of why following the steps and listening to expert advice is so crucial.

Lonnie found my team through an online lead source, and his loan process started in the traditional way. He filled out our online application, submitted his documents, and we pulled his credit report to review his options. After assessing his situation, we got him pre-qualified for a loan.

As we do with every client, we reminded Lonnie of the golden rules:

- Don't take on any new debt.
- Avoid making major financial changes (like changing jobs, getting married, or making large purchases).

Lonnie's situation had its complexities. He had switched to a lower-paying job about six months prior, and his credit was impacted by a recent divorce. Despite these challenges, Lonnie's income was stable, he had good savings, and his debts were relatively low. We determined that an FHA loan would be the best option for him.

But as we moved forward, Lonnie made several decisions that significantly impacted his loan.

First, Lonnie got married, which in Texas—a community property state—meant we had to factor in his new wife's debts, even though she wasn't on the loan. This required pulling her credit report and incorporating her financial obligations into the equation.

Then, Lonnie disclosed that he had child support obligations from his previous marriage, which hadn't come up initially. Fortunately, his child was nearing 18, so this didn't derail the process, but it added another layer of complexity and definitely more documents.

Next came the honeymoon. Lonnie and his wife spent $8,000 of their $20,000 savings during their trip, and shortly after, they opened two new credit cards to furnish their future home. So, to recap:

- He got married, triggering additional financial requirements.
- He spent nearly half of his savings.
- He incurred new debt.

- He revealed undisclosed child support obligations.

Despite these complications, this is where having a knowledgeable mortgage expert made all the difference. My team and I stepped in to tackle each issue.

We pulled his wife's credit report, consolidated his new debts through a personal loan, and worked to secure the necessary child support documentation. These adjustments weren't easy, but we managed to navigate the obstacles with minimal delay—adding only 3 to 5 extra days to the process.

In the end, Lonnie closed on his home, and we helped him overcome what could have been a deal-breaking situation.

The Lesson

Lonnie's story shows that while no home-buying journey is without its challenges, having an experienced mortgage expert on your side can help you overcome unexpected hurdles.

This doesn't mean we can always work miracles, but it does demonstrate the importance of trust, transparency, and teamwork. Following the steps and leaning on expert advice can make all the difference in achieving your dream of homeownership.

At the end of the day, we're here to ensure you have every advantage and succeed in your journey, no matter how complex the road may be.

Congratulations! You've made it through all the data points, details, and "story times" with me. I hope this has given you a clear picture of the entire process—from the very beginning stages to the final steps of buying a home. If you've purchased a home before, some of these things might be familiar. If you're a first-time buyer, I hope this helped fill in any gaps you may not have understood. Even if you're considering refinancing, much of this still applies, though refinancing has its own nuances (maybe that will be the subject of book two!). Either way, you now have more information than most people do when they buy their first home.

I want to mention that, although I've worked on loans in every state, the vast majority of my business is in Texas, where I live. While some of my stories may apply to other states, understand that the rules and processes may vary slightly. Your mortgage expert—whether it's my team or someone else—will be able to fill in any state-specific details. Keep in mind, every expert does things a little differently, so if the order of events is slightly off, that's okay. If you're unsure, don't hesitate to ask questions. A true expert won't shy away from answering them. I promise, we've heard them all before. And if you happen to ask something I don't know the answer to, my team and I will make sure to find it for you. Remember, there is no such thing as a dumb question!

I truly hope you found this information valuable and that it's given you the confidence to start your own process without stress. By understanding what you need to know, you'll be equipped to make informed decisions for you and your family. My ultimate goal is to help you reach your dreams. It doesn't matter what I or any other expert think about your goals—we're here to support you in achieving them, in the best way we know how. If you're not working with an expert who shares this approach, I encourage you to find one who does.

Thank you for joining me on this journey, and I wish you all the best as you move forward!

Chapter 14: Debunking Conventional Wisdom: What You Think is True... But It's Not!

As we wrap up this book, I want to leave you with a few common misconceptions about home loans and buying a house that you might have heard. These myths have been pushed out through marketing and advertising, but the reality is often quite different. Let's debunk some of these pieces of conventional wisdom:

Myth #1. "Interest Rate is King" - A Misleading Perception

It's easy to get swept up in the marketing frenzy around interest rates when you're shopping for a mortgage. After all, it's often touted as the single most important factor, the "king" of mortgage decisions. But is that really the case? While interest rates certainly matter, they are far from the only thing that should guide your mortgage choices—and in fact, may not even be the most critical factor.

Why, then, is the interest rate so heavily marketed? It's simple: it's easy to understand. We all get it—lower is better. So when a lender flashes a low interest rate in front of you, it's tempting to grab onto it as a clear path to saving money. But there's more at play here than meets the eye. What isn't immediately obvious is that a lower interest rate often comes with hidden costs.

If you see a lower interest rate advertised make sure to read the fine print to see all the things you need to have to qualify for this low interest rate. These qualifications typically include additional costs at the closing, a very specific credit score, a specific income amount, and several other requirements.

This additional money is sometimes referred to as "Discount Points."

Oftentimes mortgage experts are looking for something known as "the Break-Even Point." The break-even point is when the savings from your lower interest rate begins to outweigh the additional costs paid at closing to obtain the lower interest rate—might be years down the road. Yet, statistics show that the average homeowner will sell, refinance, or pay off their mortgage within 3 to 5 years. This means you could end up losing money by paying the additional costs at closing that you won't fully recoup.

Who receives the additional money that you paid to get the lower interest rate? The end investor of your loan, not your mortgage expert, collects that upfront payment. Whether you keep the loan for 3 months or 30 years, the investor has pocketed your money, and you're stuck having paid for a lower rate that you may never fully benefit from.

Why, then, is the lowest interest rate so aggressively pushed on consumers? Because it's an easy sell. As I mentioned before, the concept of "lower is better" is simple for consumers to grasp. Mortgage professionals often take the path of least resistance: it's easier for them to sell you on a low rate than to educate you on more nuanced factors that should weigh into your decision.

In reality, selecting a mortgage should be based on more than just the interest rate. It should take into account your future plans, the length of time you intend to keep the loan, and your financial goals. This is where a great mortgage expert steps in—not just to sell you the lowest rate, but to tailor the loan to your specific situation. Unfortunately, many loan officers are content to simply match a customer with the lowest rate without considering whether it makes sense for their long-term needs.

Perhaps one of the most misunderstood truths about interest rates is that they aren't as set in stone as you might think. You actually have more control over the amount of interest you'll end up paying than you realize. While the interest rate is the figure agreed upon for the full term of your loan, if you make extra payments or pay off the loan early, you will end up paying less in total interest than the original finance charge on your loan.

For example, paying just a little extra toward your mortgage each month can significantly reduce the interest you'll pay over the life of the loan. So while securing a low interest rate is certainly appealing, it's equally important to understand how your payment strategy affects the actual amount of interest you'll pay.

Rather than being seduced by the lure of a low rate, work with a mortgage expert who understands the bigger picture—someone who will guide you through a tailored approach, taking into account not only the rate but your unique needs and circumstances. The "lowest interest rate" might not always be the best deal for you, and a good mortgage expert will make sure you understand that.

Story Time: Choosing Strategy Over Rates

Let me share a story from my own life that perfectly illustrates the power of strategic decision-making in homeownership. When I bought my first home at the age of 22, I made a choice that might sound counterintuitive: I opted for an above-market interest rate instead of the lowest rate available.

Now, why would I do that?

It wasn't because I didn't care about saving on interest—I absolutely did. But at that point in my life, cash flow was my priority. I was young, had limited savings, and didn't have a lot of cash on hand for a hefty down payment or closing costs. By choosing a higher interest rate, I was able to reduce my upfront expenses and make homeownership a reality.

My goal was simple: get my foot in the door and start building equity. I understood the long-term benefits of homeownership—growing wealth through property value appreciation and maximizing tax deductions. The higher rate allowed me to achieve that while keeping my initial costs manageable.

But I didn't stop there. I knew I could control the total interest I paid over the life of the loan, so I came up with a plan. I made it a point to pay about 25% more than my scheduled mortgage payment each month, directing those extra payments toward the principal. This strategy helped me chip away at the loan balance much faster than the original 30-year term. In fact, by sticking to this plan, I would have paid off my mortgage in approximately 17 years—13 years ahead of schedule.

This experience taught me an important lesson: your mortgage is a tool, and it's how you use it that matters most. Sometimes, the best choice isn't the lowest interest rate but the one that aligns with your financial goals and circumstances. For me, the trade-off of a slightly higher rate was worth it because it got me into a home sooner and allowed me to start building equity right away.

If you approach homeownership strategically—whether by making extra payments, choosing a loan structure that works for your current situation, or refinancing when the time is right—you can create opportunities to build wealth over time. The key is to focus on what works best for your unique needs, not just what looks good on paper.

Now, I understand not everyone has the flexibility to make such significant extra payments, but even small amounts can make a big difference over time. For example, putting an additional $25-$50 per month toward your principal can drastically reduce the amount of interest you pay over the life of the loan. A great mortgage expert can help you design a strategy that aligns with your financial situation and goals, even if that means taking unconventional paths like I did. The key is to look beyond the headline interest rate and find ways to build equity and reduce costs in the long run.

So, don't underestimate the impact of even modest extra payments. By working closely with a knowledgeable mortgage expert, you can unlock creative solutions that help you get the most out of your home purchase, just like I did.

Myth #2: A Temporary Rate Buydown is a Good Financial Choice

One of the most popular products you may have heard about recently, especially as interest rates have climbed, is the temporary rate buydown. If you've been house hunting, you might have seen them advertised as an incentive, with sellers offering to "buy down" the interest rate to make the home seem more affordable. While this sounds appealing on the surface, let me explain why, in my opinion, it's more of a gimmick than a solid financial strategy for most people.

First, let's break down what a temporary rate buydown actually is. Essentially, it's a product the seller pays for that allows the buyer to enjoy a lower interest rate for the first year or two, before reverting to the standard rate. A common example is the 2/1 buydown, where your interest rate is 2% lower in year one, 1% lower in year two, and then it adjusts to the full rate for the remainder of the loan term. On the surface, this seems like a great way to soften the blow of rising interest rates. Buyers experiencing "rate sticker shock" see it as a way to get a breather on monthly payments with the hope that interest rates will drop by the time the full rate kicks in, allowing them to refinance, or that their financial situation will improve.

But here's why I believe this approach is flawed: in about 99% of cases, sellers would be better off simply reducing the price of the home by the amount it costs to fund the buydown. If you run the numbers, the total amount you save in monthly payments over the two years of the buydown often pales in comparison to the savings you'd achieve from a price reduction. In short, the math just doesn't add up to a real benefit for the buyer in most situations.

Remember what I said earlier about additional costs to gain a lower interest rate and how they rarely make sense for most buyers? The same principle applies here. The real beneficiary of this product isn't the buyer, but the investor holding your loan. The investor gets their money upfront through the buydown, regardless of how long you keep the loan.

Now, there are some cases where this product could work for a buyer. For example, if you were disciplined enough to take the money saved during the buydown period and apply it directly toward your principal balance each month, that could help offset some of the costs. But even then, you'd need to do the math carefully. In most situations, you'd probably be better off using that money to permanently reduce the interest rate by paying additional costs, if that makes sense for your specific financial goals.

This is why I don't advertise or recommend temporary rate buydowns. In my experience, they usually don't serve the buyer's best interest. If someone really wants to explore the option, I will sit down with them and go through the numbers to ensure they're making an informed decision, but I never push this product because I truly believe there are better, more sustainable financial choices for my clients.

And in case you're wondering, no, people don't use this product to qualify for a more expensive home. Why? Because mortgage guidelines require that you qualify based on the higher interest rate, not the lower introductory one. The rate that kicks in after the buydown is what's used to determine your qualification for the loan, so it doesn't actually help you afford "more house."

While I know this product is popular in certain circles, and many mortgage professionals sell it, I stand by my belief that it doesn't usually benefit the customer in the long run. My priority is helping clients build a strong financial future, and that means looking past trendy products and focusing on what truly makes sense for their life and goals.

Myth #3: ARM (Adjustable Rate Mortgages) Loans Are the Devil

Adjustable Rate Mortgages (ARMs) have developed quite a negative reputation, particularly following the housing crisis of 2008-2009. Now, don't get me wrong—ARMs aren't for everyone. In fact, in certain market conditions, like when this book is being written, ARMs rarely make sense. However, it's important to understand that they can be a great financial tool in the right circumstances, and the fear surrounding them is often based on outdated information.

First, let's address why ARMs are misunderstood. During the housing crash, many people had ARMs with terms that were indeed predatory. These loans often had very short fixed-rate periods—sometimes just one or two years—before the rates began adjusting. Worse still, they came with significant penalties for paying them off early, and even if interest rates dropped, the rate on these ARMs couldn't fall below the initial rate. On top of that, the caps on how much the interest rate could adjust were extremely high, sometimes 2-4 times higher than the caps we see on modern ARMs. These old ARM products contributed to a lot of financial pain, and as a result, they became the scapegoat for the housing market's collapse.

However, today's ARM products are much different and significantly more regulated. Most modern ARMs, particularly those referred to as "fixed-period ARMs," have a set interest rate for a specific period—usually between 3 to 7 years—before they start adjusting based on predetermined parameters. These fixed-period ARMs are often valuable when interest rates are high, but there's an expectation that they will drop in the future, or when the buyer knows they will not stay in their current mortgage for more than the fixed period.

The big advantage of ARMs is that their rates are typically lower than those of fixed-rate mortgages, especially during the initial fixed period. This can translate into substantial savings, particularly for buyers who are likely to sell, refinance, or move before the rate adjustment kicks in. As I've mentioned before, the reality is that most borrowers don't keep their mortgage for more than 3 to 5 years before they refinance, pull cash out for home improvements, or sell due to life changes such as moving for work, upgrading, or downsizing.

So, should you consider an ARM? Maybe, maybe not. The key is understanding your own financial situation and long-term goals. If you're fairly certain you won't be in your home or your mortgage for more than 5-7 years, a fixed-period ARM could save you money in interest payments.

The important thing to remember is that not all ARM loans are bad, and they certainly aren't the villain of the mortgage world. They are simply tools—loan products that serve specific customer needs. The mistake is not in offering ARM loans, but in failing to understand them and how they fit into a larger financial strategy.

The key takeaway is this: don't be afraid of ARM loans, but also don't blindly jump into one. Just because ARMs got a bad rap in the past doesn't mean they aren't useful in the right context. It's all about understanding the product, your situation, and having a knowledgeable mortgage expert who can guide you through your options.

Myth #4: You Need to Save a Specific Amount on Your Interest Rate for Refinancing to Be Worth It

You've probably heard it before—someone says that if you don't save at least 2% on your interest rate when refinancing, it's just not worth it. This myth is one of the most common, and it's also one of the most misleading. Refinancing isn't a one-size-fits-all calculation, and the amount of interest rate savings that makes refinancing "worth it" depends on a multitude of factors. Let me explain why a blanket 2% rule doesn't work.

First of all, how much you need to save for a refinance to be worth it is relative to your unique financial situation. Consider the following variables: How large is your loan? Are you taking out additional money for a project or to pay off debt? How much is it going to cost you to refinance? Are you reducing the length of time on your loan? These are just a few of the many factors that need to be weighed before deciding to refinance, and it's exactly why working with a trusted mortgage expert is so critical.

I've seen scenarios where refinancing only reduced the interest rate by 0.25%-0.5%, but it made a huge difference because there was no cost to refinance. Imagine if I told you that you could save $50, $100, or even $150 a month just by signing some paperwork and it wouldn't cost you anything. For some people, that might be an easy decision. You wouldn't have to worry about whether you're saving a full 2% on your rate—it would be a clear win based on your personal financial needs.

Story Time: Refinancing for Financial Freedom

Let me share a story that illustrates the power of homeownership and strategic refinancing. A few years ago, I helped a couple take the leap into buying their first home. At the time, they were hesitant and unsure if homeownership was the right choice for them. But after weighing the pros and cons, they decided to take the plunge.

Fast forward several years, and they reached out to me again— this time with a very different question. They had accumulated a significant amount of credit card debt and were struggling to keep up with their payments. Their financial situation had become overwhelming, and they were looking for a way to regain control.

Here's where things got tricky. Their original mortgage had an incredibly low interest rate, and refinancing would mean doubling that rate. For many people, the thought of increasing their mortgage rate might have been a dealbreaker. But instead of focusing solely on the rate, we ran the numbers to see the bigger picture.

What we discovered was eye-opening. By refinancing and rolling their high-interest credit card debt into their new mortgage, they could save over $1,000 a month. That monthly savings was life-changing for them, giving them the financial breathing room they desperately needed.

Sure, raising their mortgage rate wasn't ideal, but the overall improvement in their financial situation far outweighed that downside. Without owning their home, they would have continued to drown in credit card payments, with no viable way out.

This experience shows how powerful homeownership can be—not just as a way to build equity but also as a tool to create financial flexibility when life gets tough.

The point is, there's no magic number or rule that dictates when refinancing makes sense. It depends entirely on your circumstances. Sometimes saving just 0.5% on a mortgage with no upfront cost makes perfect sense. Other times, it might not, even if you're saving more than 2%. It's all about understanding your financial goals and situation, and that's where having someone who truly understands mortgage products is crucial.

Refinancing is not a decision to be made lightly, and it certainly shouldn't be based on conventional wisdom like "save 2% or more." Each financial situation is unique, and it's vital to work with someone who can help you weigh all the factors. This is exactly why I, and my team, stay vigilant in monitoring the market for our clients. If there's an opportunity to refinance that makes sense for you, we'll review your current mortgage for free and help you make the best decision for your financial future.

At the end of the day, the key takeaway is that you're in control of your financial decisions. There's no one-size-fits-all advice when it comes to refinancing, buying a home, or making any other major financial move. Use this book to help you ask the right questions, avoid common pitfalls, and empower yourself to take control of your financial future.

Happy house hunting, and I hope to hear from you soon!

"How to Find a Mortgage Expert" Checklist

After reading this book, you've likely realized that selecting the right mortgage expert is one of the most critical steps in buying a house. To help you make an informed choice, here's a quick rundown of how to find the right expert, along with a checklist of essential questions to guide your decision.

Mortgage experts typically work with three main types of lenders: banks/direct lenders, brokers, and correspondent (non-bank) lenders. Each has its pros and cons, and I've worked with all of them. If someone tells you there's only one "best type of lender," they're simply wrong. Let's explore why you might choose one over the other.

Key Terms:

- **Overlay**: This refers to additional restrictions beyond the basic loan guidelines. The more overlay there is, the less flexibility there is if you don't meet certain criteria.
- **Special Loan Products**: These are unique offerings, such as first-time buyer incentives or loans for specific areas.
- **Average Days to Close**: This is the average time it takes for a lender to complete the loan process once you're under contract.

Lender Types:

1. **Bank/Credit Union**: These institutions offer more than just mortgages, and may have in-house products that other lenders can't match. However, they typically have stricter overlays and longer closing times. While many assume banks offer the lowest interest rates, this isn't always true; their rates depend on their appetite for mortgages at any given time.
2. **Direct Lender**: Specializing in mortgages, direct lenders also service their loans. They often have fewer overlays than banks

but may lack special loan products. Their closing times and interest rates vary depending on the company's structure and current market conditions.

3. **Broker**: Acting as a "free agent," brokers shop around for the best loan products from various lenders. They can offer a wide range of products and generally have shorter closing times. Brokers often provide competitive rates since they can compare multiple lenders to find the best deal.

4. **Correspondent Lender**: Like brokers, correspondent lenders work with various companies but underwrite loans themselves. They offer competitive closing times and rates but may have slightly higher interest rates due to their operational costs.

I often hear mortgage professionals putting down other types of lenders, claiming their way is the only way. That's simply not true. Throughout my career, I've worked with all types of lenders—correspondent, broker, bank, and direct—and each has its pros and cons. Personally, I prefer correspondent or broker lenders for a few key reasons. First, they allow the process to flow smoothly and quickly. As an expert, I avoid overlays because they tend to create unnecessary work for both my clients and my team. I follow the KISS principle: Keep It Simple, Stupid. The mortgage process already involves gathering a lot of documents, and I prefer not to complicate it further.

Another reason I lean toward these lenders is the flexibility they offer. Not every client fits neatly into the standard mortgage criteria, and unexpected issues often arise. Having more options at my disposal allows me to handle problems efficiently. In my experience, the overall cost with correspondent or broker lenders tends to be competitive, while still offering a great deal of flexibility.

Ultimately, the choice is yours. At PBJ Mortgage, we pride ourselves on being honest with our clients. If a lender offers a special product that no one else has, I won't tell you not to go with them just for the sake of keeping your business. Instead, I'll do exactly what I'm doing here—present the pros and cons, outline any potential pitfalls, and let you make an informed decision.

A good mortgage expert isn't just focused on getting *you* through a *single* transaction, whether it's buying a house or refinancing. They're there to support you and your network through any future financial moves as well. Mortgage experts are advisers, not just people who put together some paperwork and hope it all works out.

Here are some key questions to ask when interviewing potential mortgage experts:

- What kind of lender do you work for?
- Do you specialize in any particular loan products?
- How long have you been in the industry?
- What are your average days to close?
- What do you love about your job?
- How competitive are your rates compared to the market?

I often joke that choosing the right mortgage expert is more important than just focusing on the interest rate. Here's why: too many times I've had to step in and save deals other lenders couldn't figure out. I've seen people placed in loans that didn't serve their best interests or charged with sky-high fees without any explanation. I've heard countless horror stories about clients scrambling the week of closing because their lender was disorganized or didn't calculate things correctly, causing delays or disqualification.

The reason people don't realize the importance of choosing the right mortgage expert is simple: major players in the industry have convinced everyone that the interest rate is all that matters. And while the rate is important, it's not everything. The mortgage process is far more complex, and it's my job to simplify that for you. I take the time to understand your financial dreams, what matters most to you, and what you're comfortable with. My role is not just to get you into a home but to ensure it fits your long-term financial goals.

That's why I wrote this book—to educate and empower you. If just one person reads this and gains the knowledge they need to make better financial decisions, then I've done my job.

My team and I would be honored to assist you. We'll treat you like family and guide you towards your financial goals, whatever they may be.

GLOSSARY:

Adjustable-Rate Mortgage (ARM):

An ARM is a type of mortgage where the interest rate can change periodically based on a specific financial index. ARMs typically start with a lower interest rate than fixed-rate mortgages but carry the risk of rate increases. They often have caps that limit how much the rate can change:

- Per adjustment period
- Over the life of the loan

Appraisal:

An appraisal is a professional evaluation of a property's market value. It's typically required by lenders before approving a mortgage to ensure the loan amount isn't higher than the property's value. An appraiser considers factors like the home's condition, size, location, and recent sales of comparable properties in the area.

Assets (pg 40):

This term covers all financial resources an applicant owns. It includes cash in bank accounts, investments (stocks, bonds, mutual funds), real estate, vehicles, and valuable personal property. Lenders assess assets to determine if the borrower has sufficient funds for a down payment and reserves for mortgage payments.

Certificate of Eligibility (COE):

This is an official document issued by the Department of Veterans Affairs that confirms a veteran's or service member's eligibility for a VA loan. It details the individual's service history and shows they meet the minimum service requirements for the VA loan benefit.

Clear to Close:

This status means the lender has approved all necessary documentation and the loan is ready for closing. It indicates that all conditions set by the underwriter have been met and the borrower can proceed to sign final loan documents.

Closing Costs:

These are fees and expenses, beyond the property's purchase price, that buyers and sellers incur to complete a real estate transaction. They typically range from 2% to 5% of the loan amount and may include:

- Lender fees (application, origination)
- Third-party fees (appraisal, credit report, title search)
- Government fees (recording fees, transfer taxes)
- Prepaid items (property taxes, homeowners insurance)

Conventional Loans:

These are mortgages not backed by government agencies. They conform to guidelines set by Fannie Mae and Freddie Mac. Conventional loans often require higher credit scores and larger down payments than government loans but may offer lower interest rates for well-qualified borrowers.

Debt-to-Income Ratio (DTI):

DTI is a financial measure that compares an individual's monthly debt payments to their gross monthly income, expressed as a percentage. It's a key factor lenders use to assess a borrower's ability to manage monthly payments and repay debts. There are two types:

- Front-end DTI: Includes only housing-related debts.
- Back-end DTI: Includes all monthly debt payments.

Lenders typically prefer a DTI of 43% or lower for qualified mortgages.

Dependents:

These are individuals, usually children or elderly relatives, who rely on the loan applicant for financial support. Lenders consider dependents because they impact the applicant's financial obligations, potentially affecting their ability to repay the loan.

Discount Points:

Discount points are fees you can choose to pay upfront to lower your mortgage interest rate.

1. How do they work?

- You pay money now to save money later.
- Each point typically costs 1% of your loan amount.
- In return, your interest rate is reduced, the amount is determined by what the market is bearing.

2. Simple example:

- Let's say you're borrowing $300,000.
- One point would cost $3,000 (1% of $300,000).
- How many points you will be asked to pay and how much lower your interest payment will be, will depend on what the mortgage market is doing at that moment in time.

4. Why consider them?

- If you plan to stay in the home for a long time, you might save more in interest over the life of the loan than you paid for the points.

5. Is it always a good idea?

- Not necessarily. It depends on how long you plan to keep the mortgage.
- You need to calculate the "break-even point" - how long it takes for the savings to exceed what you paid to reduce the interest rate.

6. Key takeaway:

- Discount points are a trade-off: pay more upfront to pay less over time.

Remember, whether discount points are a good deal depends on your specific financial situation and long-term plans. It's always a good idea to run the numbers and consult with a mortgage expert before deciding.

Earnest Money Deposit:

This is a good faith deposit made by a buyer to show they're serious about purchasing a property. It's usually a percentage of the purchase price and is held in escrow. If the sale goes through, it's typically applied to the down payment or closing costs.

Escrow:

An escrow is a financial arrangement where a third party holds and regulates payment of funds or assets on behalf of two parties in a transaction. In real estate, it's commonly used in two ways:

a) During a home purchase: An escrow account holds the buyer's earnest money deposit until the sale is completed.

b) As part of a mortgage: An escrow account collects a portion of monthly mortgage payments to cover property taxes and insurance premiums.

FHA Loan:

This government-backed loan is insured by the Federal Housing Administration. It offers lower down payments (as low as 3.5%) and is more forgiving of lower credit scores, making it popular with first-time homebuyers.

Fixed-Rate Mortgage:

This is a mortgage loan where the interest rate remains the same for the entire term of the loan. Benefits include:

- Predictable monthly payments
- Protection against rising interest rates
- Easier budgeting and financial planning
- However, borrowers won't benefit if market rates fall unless they refinance.

Government Loans:

These are mortgages backed by government agencies, designed to make homeownership more accessible. They often have more lenient credit requirements and lower down payments than conventional loans. Examples include FHA, VA, and USDA loans.

Hard Pull:

Also known as a "hard inquiry," this occurs when a lender checks your credit report as part of the loan application process. It can temporarily lower your credit score by a few points and remains on your credit report for about two years.

Homeowners Insurance (HOI):

This is a type of property insurance that covers losses and damages to an individual's house and assets in the home. It typically provides both interior and exterior coverage and may protect against theft, fire, and some natural disasters. Mortgage lenders usually require borrowers to maintain HOI as a condition of the loan.

Individual or Joint Credit:

This refers to how a loan application is submitted. Individual credit means one person applies for the loan and is solely responsible for repayment. Joint credit involves two or more people applying together, sharing responsibility for repayment. This is common for couples or business partners buying property together.

Initial Closing Disclosure:

This document provides the final details about the mortgage loan, including the exact interest rate, monthly payments, and itemized closing costs. It must be provided to the borrower at least three business days before closing, allowing time for review.

Loan Estimate:

This standardized form provides details about the terms of a mortgage loan, including the estimated interest rate, monthly payment, and closing costs. Lenders must provide this within three business days of receiving a loan application.

Loan-to-Value Ratio (LTV):

LTV is a lending risk assessment ratio that financial institutions and other lenders examine before approving a mortgage. It's calculated as:

LTV = (Mortgage Amount / Appraised Property Value) x 100

Marital Status:

In lending, this indicates whether an applicant is single, married, separated, divorced, or widowed. It's important because it can affect property rights, especially in community property states where spouses may have a legal claim to assets even if they're not on the loan.

MLS (Multiple Listing Service) drip:

This is an automated system that sends potential buyers regular updates about new property listings that match their specified criteria. It helps keep interested buyers informed about available properties without requiring manual searches.

Non-Conforming Loans:

These mortgages don't meet the standards set by Fannie Mae and Freddie Mac, often because they exceed the maximum loan amount (jumbo loans) or don't meet other criteria. They may have different terms and interest rates compared to conforming loans.

PMI (Private Mortgage Insurance):

This insurance protects the lender if a borrower defaults on a conventional loan with a down payment of less than 20%. The borrower pays PMI premiums, typically until they reach 20% equity in the home.

Pre-Qualification:

This is an initial step in the mortgage process where a lender provides an estimate of how much you might be able to borrow. It's based on self-reported information about your income, assets, and debts, without verifying the information or checking your credit report.

Pre-Approval:

This is a more rigorous process than pre-qualification. The lender verifies your financial information, checks your credit, and issues a conditional commitment to loan a specific amount. This gives you a clear idea of your budget and shows sellers you're a serious buyer.

Refinancing:

This is the process of replacing an existing mortgage with a new one, typically to achieve one or more of the following:

- Lower interest rate

- Lower monthly payments
- Shorter loan term
- Convert from an adjustable-rate to a fixed-rate mortgage (or vice versa)
- Access home equity

Soft Pull):

This is a credit check that doesn't affect your credit score. It's often used for pre-qualification or when you check your own credit. Soft pulls don't require your permission and aren't visible to other lenders reviewing your credit report.

Title:

This legal document establishes the owner's right to possess and use the property. It includes a description of the property and any encumbrances, such as mortgages or easements. A clear title is crucial for real estate transactions.

Title Insurance:

This insurance protects the lender and/or homeowner against issues with the property's title, such as unknown liens, forgeries, or errors in public records. It's typically required by lenders and offers peace of mind to buyers.

USDA Loan:

This program, backed by the United States Department of Agriculture, is designed to promote homeownership in rural areas. It offers no-down-payment mortgages to eligible buyers in specified rural locations.

VA Loan:

This loan program, guaranteed by the Department of Veterans Affairs, is available to eligible veterans, active-duty service members, and surviving spouses. It often requires no down payment and has competitive interest rates.

Resources

Helpful Checklists can be found using this QR Code: